金森 強

編著

CLIL
で習得する
小学校英語指導
の基礎

ミネルヴァ書房

は じ め に

　2019年度から小学校教員養成課程に外国語（英語）のコアカリキュラムに応じた教育課程が置かれるようになって既に４年が経ちました。小学校教員の養成を行う多くの大学のカリキュラムに外国語活動（中学年）・外国語科（高学年）の学習，指導，評価に関する基本的な知識や指導技術を身につけるための科目として，（１）「外国語の指導法（２単位程度)」，小学校における外国語活動・外国語科の授業実践に必要な実践的な英語運用能力に関する背景的な知識を身につける科目として，（２）「外国語に関する専門的事項（１単位程度)」の二つが置かれているはずです。

　（１）は，授業実践に必要な知識・理解を目指しており，その内容としては，①「小学校外国語教育についての基本的な知識・理解」，②「子供の第二言語習得についての知識とその活用」，および，授業実践：「指導技術」，「授業作り」となっており，「授業の観察」，「授業体験」，「模擬授業」を体験しながら身につけることがねらいとなっています。

　（２）については，外国語活動・外国語科の授業を担当するために必要な実践的な英語運用能力を，授業場面を意識しながら身につけるための科目であり，５領域にわたる英語力に加えて，①「英語に関する基本的な知識（音声，語彙，文構造，文法，正書法等)」，②「第二言語習得に関する基本的な事項についての理解」，③「児童文学（絵本，子供向けの歌や詩等）についての理解」，④「異文化理解に関する事項」についての理解があげられています。

　（１）の「外国語の指導法（２単位程度)」用テキストは既に多数存在するようですが，（２）「外国語に関する専門的事項（１単位程度)」用テキストはあまり目にしたことがありません。本書は，（２）の授業用テキストとして作成されたものです。教員養成学部に勤務する，各分野に造詣の深い研究者が，予想される受講生の実態や興味・関心を踏まえた上で執筆にあたりました。内容が

専門的になりすぎないように努めてはいますが，若干難しくなっている部分も
あるかもしれません。また，分かりやすさを優先したため十分な説明になって
いないところもあるかもしれませんが，その点は，ご容赦いただければと思い
ます。

　限られた授業時数で本テキストを効果的にご利用いただくために，ミニ・レ
クチャーのパートは，事前・事後の学習課題として使用して頂くことをお勧め
します。クラスルームイングリッシュにも早い段階から声に出して慣れ親しん
でおくことが望まれます。付属の音源を用いて練習し，受講者同士で確認した
り，アドバイスし合ったりする活動を通して，仲間と一緒に成長する協働的な
学習体験としてご利用頂くと良いのではないでしょうか。

　小学校で英語に出会う子どもたちの指導にあたる受講生たちが，自信を持っ
て教壇に立てるように，本書が，必要となる知識・技能の習得に少しでも役に
立てることを願っています。

　最後に，本書を出版するにあたっては，株式会社ミネルヴァ書房の長田亜里
沙さんに大変お世話になりました。長田さんの丁寧で巧みな手綱さばきがなけ
れば，本書の上梓は幻に終わったかもしれません。改めて感謝の気持ちをお伝
えしたいと思います。

2023年12月

著者代表　金森　強

CLIL で習得する　小学校英語指導の基礎

目　次

はじめに

Track について

本書では，🎧Track の音源を YouTube で視聴することができます。

●視聴方法

①🎧Track で示されている二次元バーコードを，カメラ付き携帯電話などで読み取ります（読み取り方法は，携帯電話の機種によって異なります。ご不明な点につきましては，各メーカーにお問い合わせください）。

②音源が掲載されている YouTube サイトの URL が表示されるので，クリックするとアクセスできます。※下のミネルヴァ書房ホームページ内の URL からも視聴が可能です。

③画面の再生ボタンを押し，音源を視聴します。

（注意）

・音源の著作権は，著作者およびミネルヴァ書房に帰属します。動画の一部または全部を無断で複製，転載，改変，配布，販売することは禁止いたします。ご不明な点は，ミネルヴァ書房までお問い合わせください。

・音源の再生や視聴にあたってはデータ通信を行うため，通信料が発生します。発生したデータ通信費用につきましては視聴者のご負担となります。

・音源の視聴にあたっては生じた損害につきましては，責任を負いかねます。ご了承ください。

解答について

本書の問題の解答は，下のミネルヴァ書房ホームページ内で，パスワードを入力するとダウンロードすることができます。【パスワード】Answer_097081

自身で問題を解いた後に確認し，学びを深めましょう。

『CLIL で習得する　小学校英語指導の基礎』補助教材のお知らせ▶
https://www.minervashobo.co.jp/news/n56571.html

Unit 1
World Englishes

1 Warm-up Activities

A Choose the correct meaning for the following words or phrases using (1) to (10) below.

(　) Englishes 　(　) accent 　(　) creole 　(　) accuracy
(　) comprehensible 　(　) pidgin 　(　) loan words 　(　) fluency
(　) mother tongue 　(　) Singlish

---

1 . varieties of English：「英語には複数の種類がある」という概念

2 . to be able to understand：理解できる

3 . a way of pronunciation that shows where a person is from：なまり

4 . a simple form of language used with a local language：混成語

5 . a language formed when a pidgin becomes a first language：混成言語

6 . the ability to do something without making mistakes：正確さ

7 . the ability of using a language easily：流暢さ

8 . the first language that you speak as a child：母国語

9 . a word from another language used in its original form：借用語

10. a type of English spoken in Singapore：シングリッシュ

B Read the following sentences, and check the box in front of each sentence that describes you.

☐ 1 . I like the English language.

☐ 2 . I like studying the English language.

☐ 3 . I do not like my English accent.

☐ 4 . All Japanese people should learn the English language.

☐ 5 . Japanese should learn American English.

□ 6. Accuracy is more important than fluency when learning a language.

□ 7. Traveling abroad is the best way to learn the English language.

2 Aural & Oral Activities

[A] Read the questions below. Then listen to Track 1-1 and decide whether each sentence is True (T) or False (F) according to the conversation.

1. The store has an English menu. T/F

2. When a word is translated, the word may lose its meaning. T/F

3. People are not touched by English vocabulary. T/F

4. Japlish is not a word made by combining Japanese and English. T/F

5. A standard in a language is hard to define. T/F

[B] Listen again and fill in the blanks.   🎧Track 1-1 ▶

Steve : Is there an English menu?

Rie :   Here's one.

Steve : Is this the English menu? I don't understand anything. Ebi-nigiri, Norimaki, Kappa-maki… What does this all mean?

Rie :   I know! It is the English menu, but it is ¹(   ).

Steve : I guess some words aren't actually translated because they lose their ²(   ) connotations.

Rie :   I am actually learning about this in school. The class is called ³(   ) Englishes.

Steve : Englishes?

Rie :   Haven't heard of Englishes? Many people in the world use English and they add their own touch to it.

Steve : Oh, I get it. You are saying this is Japanese English.

Rie :   Yes, or Japlish. But I never heard it called that way ⁴(   ).

Steve : Come to think of it, I have heard of Singlish. My Singaporean friend said something in English, but I couldn't ⁵(   ).

Rie :   What did he say?

Steve : He said "Confirm plus chop" which uses all English words. It means "Yes, I'm sure."

Rie :   That reminds me of Hawaiian Pidgin. Like when a local says 'da kine' for things they can't remember.

Steve : Sounds like 'the kind'.

Rie :   Right, but wait. Second ⁶(   ) use it as a first language, so maybe it is a creole, and not a pidgin.

Steve : Languages are so interesting. It makes you think about what '⁷(   )' means.

C̲ Let's try 'Role-Play Shadowing'.

1 . Listen to the Track and check the pronunciation and meaning of each word and sentence.

2 . Try 'Role-Play Shadowing' using the Track with a partner.

3 . Change roles and repeat.

4 . Now role-play with a partner without the Track. Be sure to focus on using the appropriate intonation, rate of utterance, and tone of voice.

D̲ Talk with a partner, and take turns asking and answering the following questions. Then, change partners, and ask and repeat.

1 . What Japanese English do you know?

2 . Which variety of the English language did you hear the most in school?

3 . In what situation have you used the English language outside of school?

4 . In what country would you like to study the English language?

5 . What is most important to learn the English language effectively?

3 Reading Part

A Vocabulary and Phrases

① concentric circles 同心円　② represents 表す

③ encompass 取り囲む　④ trade 商業，商い

⑤ distinct 他とまったく別な　⑥ official 公用

⑦ monolingual 一か国語だけ用いた　⑧ multilingual 多数の国語を用いた

⑨ expose さらす　⑩ evolving 発展する

B True or False Questions

　Read the following statements. After you have read the passage below, answer whether the sentences are True (T) or False (F) according to the passage.

1 . There are more native speakers in the world than second language speakers. T/F

2 . 'Lingua Franca' means first language in English. T/F

3 . English is a pidgin in the Philippines. T/F

4 . English is studied as a foreign language in Japan. T/F

5 . Other languages are making changes to English. T/F

C Multiple Choice

　After you have read the passage below, circle the correct statements in each group.

1 . a. Most English speakers are from the inner circle.

　　b. Most English speakers are from the outer circle.

　　c. Most English speakers are from the expanding circle.

2 . a. Lingua franca is used to conquer a country.

　　b. Lingua franca is used as a communication tool.

　　c. Lingua franca was developed by the French.

3 . a. Many people use English only with native speaker culture.

　　b. Many people use English only with their own culture.

　　c. Many people use English with both their own and other cultures.

4 . a. There will be new English words in the inner circle.

　　b. There will be no new Englishes in the future.

　　c. There will be a mixture of many different Englishes in the future.

5 . a. We should learn only native Englishes.

　　b. We should learn a variety of Englishes.

　　c. We should learn a variety of Englishes and their cultures.

4　Reading Activities

 Track 1-2 ▶

Read the following sentences. Listen to the Track, and read it again.

The Three Circles

Three concentric circles are often used to understand how the English language is used in different countries. The inner circle represents the native speakers of English, such as the United Kingdom, the United States, and Australia. Next is the outer circle. It includes countries whose mother tongue is not English, but it plays an important role in the country and is sometimes used as an official language. The outer circle includes countries such as India, Nigeria, and the Philippines. Finally, the expanding circle encompasses countries where English is not an official language, but it is studied by most people and widely

concentric circles 同心円

represents 表す

official 公用

encompass 取り囲む

used as a foreign language in communication situations among speakers of different languages. These countries include most of Europe and many Asian countries.

English is now considered a lingua franca. It is a word with Italian origin which means a trade language or common language. In other words, it refers to the language used when people who speak different languages are communicating. It is sometimes called a third language that is distinct from the speakers' mother tongues. It is also used in contexts ignoring inner circle culture which is the main reason the English language is evolving, and new Englishes are created.

How should teachers, especially in the expanding circle, teach the English language? Perhaps, they should provide learners with an overview of the many types of Englishes throughout the globe. Teachers should also teach the clear distinction between monolingual and multilingual situations. They should also have their students learn about mixing and switching back and forth between languages. This instruction can be done by exposing students to a variety of Englishes.

trade 商業, 商い

distinct 他とまったく別な

evolving 発展する

monolingual 一か国語だけ用いた
multilingual 多数の国語を用いた
expose さらす

5 Mini Lectures

1. 国際共通語としての英語

言葉は変わるもの

　言語はなぜ生まれたのでしょう。それは，私たちが意思伝達をするためです。中でも「英語」は今や世界共通語として世界中で話されています。しかし，私たち日本人がこの英語を使う場合，それは純然たる英語とは呼べません。なぜならそこには日本独自の文化，言語感覚，生活環境が否応なく介在してくるからです。英語は，それを使う人の興味・関心，歴史的背景，日常生活，その他あらゆる物事の影響を受けてしまいます。世界のグローバル化にともなって，英語は今以上に世界中へと広がっていきます。つまり，より多くの人間が英語を使うことにより，英語は益々彼らの影響を受けて新しくなっていくのです。

　これは何も近年見られる現象ではありません。元々英語はこのように成り立ってきました。例えば，17世紀，ヨーロッパから新しい土地にやって来たアメリカ入植者たちは，新天地で数多くの新しい物事に出会いました。初めて目にした植物，動物，人々，それらにまつわる数々の言葉と遭遇しました。これにより，徐々にイギリス英語から分離したアメリカ英語というものが形成されていきました。言葉と言葉が出会って新たな言葉が生まれる，この過程には数日しかかかりません。例えば，入植者が出会ったネイティブ・アメリカンの語彙「アボガド」「スカンク」「ティーピー」，これらはまさに一瞬のうちに変化し定着した言葉の代表です。英語にはこのように，元々その土地に根付いていた言葉を発祥とする語彙が豊富にあるのです。これを「借用語」と呼びます。

　あなたが日頃，英語由来と思っている言葉の中にも，この「借用語」が多く存在していることでしょう。一例を挙げると，南アフリカのある交差点には，「ROBOT AHEAD」という看板が立っていますが，この「ROBOT」は人間の形をしたお馴染みの機械を指しているわけではありません。ここでいう「ロボット」は「信号機」を意味しているのです。無論イギリスやアメリカ英語にこのような概念は存在しません。しかしこの土地では「機械」という意味でこの語が使われてきました。つまり言葉を「借用」しているわけです。また，そもそもこの「ロボット」という言葉自体，本来英語由来ではありません。この語は

チェコ語の「robota」という言葉を英語が「借用」したものです。

日本語由来の英語

　英語は世界中の国々で使われていますが，必ずしも母語，つまり第一言語として使用されているとは限りません。生活するために必要な第二言語（English as a Second Language：ESL）として使ったり，あるいは，外国語（English as a Foreign Language：EFL）として学んだ言語として使われるケースも少なくありません。実際，英語を話す全人口のうち，このEFLの使用者の割合が最も多いとされています。そのため，英語を使う人々の母語が，何らかの形で英語に影響を与えてしまうのです。日本語はそのいい例です。オタク，オリガミ，エダマメ，これらは近年，英語使用者の間で多く使われている言葉です。日本のみで使われていた言葉を，来日した英語話者が母国に持ち帰り使い始めます。使用頻度が高くなるにつれ英語辞典にも載り始めます。Typhoon, karaoke, sushiはその代表的な言葉です。また，日本文化が英語で説明される時はそのままの日本語が使われ，日本語英語と呼ばれることもあります。その代表的なものがよく知られる「おもてなし」です。この語は和英辞書では「hospitality」と出てきます。さらに英英辞典では「ホストがゲストを飲食やエンタテインメントで楽しませること」と説明されています。しかし，これだけでは「相手のために敬意を込めてもてなす」という日本特有のニュアンスまで知ることができません。そこで，「I will do hospitality.」を訳してみます。しかし，この文では，英語話者は日本の「おもてなし」の心を理解できない可能性が高くなります。英文法的に正確であっても，意味するところのニュアンスが微妙に違ってくるからです。一方で，このことは，英語話者に「おもてなし」の意味を考えるきっかけを与えることになります。実際に日本でおもてなしを経験したり，経験者から英語で「omotenashi」の意味を聞いたりすることにより，徐々にその言葉が英語ではうまく説明できないことに気づきます。こうして「I will do omotenashi.」という代替えの効かない表現が成り立っていくのです。このように英語は，世界中のいたるところで各地の文化的な影響を受けながら語彙を増やし，新しくなっていきます。

2．中間言語を大切に

言語をアップデートしていく

　異なる母国語を持つ者同士が会話をする際，英語が用いられるケースはよくあります。ただし，そこでは，英語を母国語とする人から見れば，明らかに不適切と思える文法や発音が含まれることも少なくありません。また，英語圏の文化や習慣を無視し，話者の母語や文化，個人の価値観に基づいて，本来の意味や使用法とは異なる英語の使用が起こっているケースも見られます。それでも，互いの意思疎通の点においては問題があるわけではありません。

　言葉の習得は，文法や語彙をすべて理解，記憶してから使い始めていくわけではありません。新しい語を学び，使用するうちに，徐々に言語はアップデートされていき，身についていくのです。このように，言語習得の途中段階で身に付けている言語能力を「中間言語」と呼びます。この中間言語は，言語を身に付ける過程で誰もが持つことになるものです。中間言語とは，言語使用者の内面にある言語能力や言語感覚を表すものであると考えられます。

　日本人が英語でコミュニケーションを図ろうとする場合も同様です。元から備わっている日本の文化，言語の感覚を通して，新たに身に付けている英語を使用することになります。中間言語は，使用者各自が持つ個人の言語経験を通して構成されていきます。日本人英語学習者は，教師の指導や個人的な学習を通して取得し，文法や発音などのルールを作り，自ら改良を重ねていくことになります。例えば，「私はそれを食べられません。」と伝えたい場合，初段回では「I don't eat.」と発し，学習中のどこかで「I can't eat.」に変わり，徐々に「I can't eat it.」へと変化していくでしょう。

中間言語の特徴

　中間言語の特徴として五つの要素が挙げられます。まず，学習段階における要因として，①ルールの過剰一般化，②学習方略，③学習時の転移の三つがあります。①は，上述した過去形の「-ed」使用例のことです。②は，知っている言葉のみで意思伝達を図ろうすることです。例えば，まだ十分に進行形を習得できていない学習者が「I am eating my lunch.」ではなく「I am eat my lunch.」

9

と表現するということです。③は，文法事項などを教師が誤って教える，あるいは学習者が無意識に誤った文法を覚えることにより，間違った認識が植え付けられることです。

　残りの二つは，母語の影響を受ける場合です。それは，④母語からの言語干渉，⑤コミュニケーション方略です。④の「言語干渉」には正と負の両方に働くという特徴があります。例えば，日本語には「〜している」という現在進行形のルールがあり，これが英語の「be動詞＋〜ing」を習得させやすくしています。一方で，日本語には「r」と「l」の区別がないため，これらの発音の違いを習得しづらくなっている，といった具合です。⑤は，コミュニケーションを図る際に起こる問題の対処のことです。会話中，適当な単語が出てこない場合，別の単語に置き換えたりする現象が起きます。例えば「床」を表現したい時「floor」という単語が出てこず，外来語である「ground」を代わりに使うことで対処します。これらを考え合わせると，教師の最大の役割は，学習者が各自の中間言語を最適な形で更新していけるよう手助けをすることです。

必要な手立てを効果的に

　さてここで，教師の役割について考えてみましょう。教師は，生徒がこの中間言語を理解し，アップデートしていける学習環境を与えなければなりません。よく引き合いに出されるのが過去形の事例です。学習者は過去を表すため，語尾を「-ed」にすることをまず学ぶでしょう。すると最初はあらゆる動詞に「ed」を用いてしまいます。つまりwentやateであるべきところを，goedやeatedとしてしまうのです。教師はこのような事例を承知しておき，教室で彼らが自ら誤りに気づき正確な語彙へと更新できる場面を設けてあげる必要があります。そのためには，学習者が取得した語彙をインプット，アウトプットする活動の機会を十分に用意し言語活動において使用しながら気づかせてあげることが大切です。単発的な訂正や説明，正しい英文を暗記させることに終始するのを避けるということです。表面的な修正だけに頼ってしまうと定着が起こらない場合があります。例えば，教室では正確に「He went there yesterday.」と使うかもしれませんが，一歩外に出ると「彼はどこに行きましたか」という質問に

対し，「He goed there.」と発言してしまうかもしれません。自身で気づかせるためには，多くのインプットを提供することに加えて，会話においては，学習者の間違いを指摘するのではなく，正しい英語表現を繰り返して Recast する（教師が「He went there yesterday.」と言う）ことを通して学習者自身に気づかせ，修正するように促す機会を作ってあげることが大切になります。

3.　これからの英語
リンガ・フランカとしての英語の存在

　世界で英語を使う人の数は20億と推定されます。この英語使用者の人口は，同心円モデルで表現されます。内円は英語を母国語として使う人口を表し，その数は約 4 億人です。外円は ESL の人口を表しており，ここにはインドやフィリピンを始め最低でも60か国が入ってきます。推定値で 7 億人とされています。さらに一番外周の拡大円には，日本も含む EFL の人口が表されます。その人口はおよそ 1 億人から10億人とされています。これは初心者から上級者まで含まれており，推定数は日々変動しています。

　現代において，英語は多くの人々に用いられ世界的に見て多大な影響力を持つ言語となっています。歴史的に見れば，19世紀に大英帝国が政治や経済において世界規模の力を握ったことで，産業や科学の言語は英語になりました。やがて20世紀にアメリカが力を握ったことにより英語は急速に世界中に広まりグローバル展開を見せました。国際的な金融機関は米ドルを中心に動いてきました。今や，映画や音楽などサブカルチャーの中心で英語は日常的に使われ，最もポピュラーな言語として定着しています。このように，英語は世界中の人々の豊かな生活に貢献しており，リンガ・フランカとして国際補助言語の役割を果たしていると言えます。そして，この状況は当面変わらないとされています。

言語は時代や文化を映す

　言語というものは変わり続けるものです。具体的にどこがどう変化するかまでは予測できませんが，変わっていくことに違いはありません。このような言語の特性を考えるとある一つの事実が見えてきます。それは，表面上，語彙や

表現を理解できたとしても，その背後にある真の意味まで把握するのは難しい，ということです。つまり，話者が伝えようとするメッセージを真の意味で理解するには，話者の持つ文化的背景まで理解する必要があるからです。

　例えば，ペットを飼っていない孫が「My dog was bad.」と発話するのを聞いた祖父は解釈に困るでしょう。これを直訳すると「私の犬は悪かった」になりますが，アメリカの若い世代の間で「dog」は「ダチ（友達）」，「bad」は「良い」の意味を持つスラング（俗語）になっているので，「あいつはかっこよかった！」というメッセージになります。このように，同じ国の母語話者同士であっても語句の意味の違いや発音が微妙に異なったりすることから，互いの英語を理解できなかったりすることは起こり得るのです。

　また，日本の家庭に招かれた外国人が驚くこととして，何もお願いしていないのに「Here you are. Japanese tea.」と，どこの家に行っても笑顔で緑茶（夏は麦茶に変わる）が出されることがあります。日本のおもてなしとして，客に「お茶を出す」ということは最も基本的なことなのかもしれませんが，欧米であれば，「Would you like something to drink?」「What would you like to drink?」等と，客が飲みたい飲み物を出すことを良しとする欧米の文化との違いがあります。

　文化を学ぶことの重要性はここにあります。日本人英語使用者にとっては，英語の理解のみに留まらず，日本語や日本文化について伝えていくことも，とても大切な能力だと言えるのです。

規範文法と記述文法

　英語の場合だけではなく，日本語においても同様です。言語は生き物のように流動的であり，変化し続けています。これを鑑みると言語に対して「正確な」という形容動詞は相応しくないのかもしれません。実際，文法的なルールは変化が遅くても語彙や表現の持つ意味は想像以上に速いペースで変化しているからです。年配者が「最近の若者の日本語はおかしい」という場面をしばしば目にしますが，その人は言語が変化するという事実をよく理解できていないのかもしれません。年配者自身，未だに「〜でござる」を使っていたりはしないは

ずです。

このような食い違いが起きる現象を，規範文法と記述文法の違いで説明することができます。規範文法とは，「言語はどうあるべきか」という考え方です。例えば，「『全然』は否定を表現する時だけ用いる」，英語であれば，「分離不定詞の『to quickly go』と用いるのは間違いだ」のような指摘は規範文法の視点からきたものです。一方，記述文法とは，その言語を使う人が日常的に作り出す言語をそのまま記述する考え方です。「全然大丈夫」と使っても，指摘を受けることは珍しくなりました。英語の分離不定詞も同様に目鯨を立てて正されることはほぼなくなってきています。これは，記述文法の視点から言葉を見ているからです。言語教師は，どちらかが「正しい」という見方だけではなく，両方の視点から言語を見ることが必要であることも大切なのです。

6 Summary & Reflection

A Summary

Here is a brief summary of the readings. Fill in the blanks to check your comprehension.

All languages develop and change based on the needs of its users. English is no exception. The term [1](   ) refers to differences in English that are used in different situations all over the world. Because a society has various needs, many varieties of English now exist. These include British English, Indian English, Singaporean English, and even [2](   )

A new English emerges as people use it to adapt to their situation. For instance, English users from the expanding circle adapt English to suit their own needs and culture which is called [3](   ). For example, an izakaya is sometimes called 'pub' in English, but it does not capture all the nuances of what an izakaya really is! Thus, even in English, it is not translated and called izakaya. It may soon enter the American English vocabulary as a [4](   ).

The different versions of English can be in the user's spelling, pronunciation, and grammar. These adaptations come together over time as a new English develops in a specific situation. Among the ⁵(   ) the outer circle has the largest population. In other words, there are more people studying and using English in the world than there are native speakers. Thus, in the future the English language will change, and new ones will be developed.

B Reflection

　本章では，世界の英語について学んできました。世界の英語に関する以下の語句について，具体的な例をあげながら説明してみましょう。

	語　　句	説　　明
1	World Englishes 世界の英語	
2	Loan Words 借用語	
3	Three Concentric Circles 同心円モデル	
4	Internalization 内在化	
5	Japanese English 日本人英語	

Unit **2**
Second Language Acquisition

1 Warm-up Activities

[A] Choose the correct meaning for the following words or phrases using (1)
to (10) below.

(   ) niece   (   ) environment   (   ) foreign   (   ) study

(   ) master   (   ) recommend   (   ) bilingual   (   ) provide

(   ) dialect   (   ) stage

---

1 . a form of a language used in one region or a social class：方言

2 . one part of the progress of something：段階

3 . having and using two languages：二言語使用者　二言語使用能力のある

4 . to learn how to do something well：習得する

5 . to say something is good and useful：勧める

6 . belonging to a country that is not yours：外国の

7 . the daughter of your brother or sister：姪

8 . the conditions in which you live, work, or play：環境

9 . to give something to somebody：与える，提供する

10. scientific research into a subject or a book or article：研究，研究論文

[B] Read the following sentences, and check the box in front of each sentence
that describes you.

☐ 1 . I do not use dialects. I use standard Japanese without any accent.

☐ 2 . I remember the first word I said when I was a baby.

☐ 3 . I want to be bilingual.

☐ 4 . I want to know how to become a bilingual or a multilingual person.

☐ 5 . When I was a child, I was poor at pronouncing *mayonnaise*.

□ 6 . We must speak at least two languages in the 21st century.

□ 7 . Children should learn foreign languages as early as possible.

2 Aural & Oral Activities

[A] Read the questions below. Then listen to Track 2-1 and decide whether each sentence is True (T) or False (F) according to the conversation.

1 . Rie has a picture of her brother's son. T/F

2 . Rie's brother was so surprised that the baby spoke two languages. T/F

3 . The professor believes the first word was 'mama'. T/F

4 . Rie's brother is bilingual. He speaks Spanish, too. T/F

5 . Rie will recommend her brother to take her niece to a bilingual school. T/F

[B] Listen again and fill in the blanks.　　　　　Track 2-1 ▶

Rie :　Look at this picture. She is my brother's baby,
　　　my niece Yui. She is so cute, right?

Steve : Oh, yes. She has a nice smile. How old is she?

Rie :　She is eleven months old.

Steve : Really? Does she speak yet?

Rie :　Yes, the first word she said was 'papa'. Can you believe it?

Steve : Hum…., that's good, but I'm [1]( ) she didn't say 'papa'.

Rie :　She often uses [2]( ) one word, like 'Daddy'. for "Daddy is sleeping.", "Daddy is not here." or "Play with me, daddy."

Steve : She is in the 'one-word stage', now.

Rie :　Would it be a good idea to [3]( ) teaching foreign languages to my niece now?

Steve : Yes, some studies have shown the younger they start learning a foreign language, the [4]( ) it is for them to master it.

Rie :　I see. I will tell my brother to start bilingual [5]( ).

Steve : They should provide an appropriate bilingual environment for your niece. Does your brother or his wife speak a foreign language?

Rie : No..., ⁶(　　　　　) them speak only Japanese.

Steve : Then, you should ⁷(　　　　　) them to choose a good bilingual school.

[C] Let's try 'Role-Play Shadowing'.

1 . Listen to the Track and check the pronunciation and meaning of each word and sentence.

2 . Try 'Role-Play Shadowing' using the Track with a partner.

3 . Change roles and repeat.

4 . Now role-play with a partner without the Track. Be sure to focus on using the appropriate intonation, rate of utterance, and tone of voice.

[D] Talk with a partner, and take turns asking and answering the following questions. Then, change partners, and ask and repeat.

1 . Which foreign country and foreign language do you like? Why?

2 . What was the first word you said to your family?

3 . What would you like your last words to be before crossing over?

4 . What do you want to do when you master English?

5 . What do you think is the best way to learn a foreign language?

3 Reading Part

[A] Vocabulary and Phrases

① newborn baby 新生児　② caretaker 保護者　③ official language 公用語

④ vowel 母音　⑤ with possible exceptions 例外の可能性はあっても

⑥ hypothesis 仮説　⑦ consonant 子音

⑧ a biologically specified period 生物学的に特定された時期

⑨ acquire 獲得する　⑩ language acquisition device 言語習得装置

⑪ exposure 浸す　⑫ provided with 与えられる　⑬ circumstance 状況

⑭ language interference 言語干渉　⑮ target language 目標言語

B True or False Questions

　Read the following statements. After you have read the passage below, answer whether the sentences are True (T) or False (F) according to the passage.

1. Newborn babies learn their language in their school with the help of teachers. T/F

2. In India, English is a foreign language, and people have many common languages. T/F

3. English can be the second language for some children in Japan. T/F

4. The LAD allows us to learn only one language in a critical or sensitive period. T/F

5. Japanese children cannot be bilingual because we use Chinese letters to learn subjects. T/F

6. First language interference influences the incorrect use of a students' foreign language. T/F

7. Language teachers with knowledge of SLA can teach a language better. T/F

C Multiple Choice

　After you have read the passage below, circle the correct statements in each group.

1. a. Newborn babies can speak a language, but they can say just one word.

　b. Newborn babies cannot speak a language, but they can understand the caretakers' language.

　c. Newborn babies cannot speak a language. They need about one year to say a word.

2. a. In India, people use English as their first language.

b. In India, people must use more than three languages.

c. In India, people use English because it is the common language of the country.

3 . a. The sensitive period is a period for babies to master cooking skills.

b. After the sensitive period, babies can learn languages with ease.

c. Before the sensitive period, it is easy for babies to learn languages.

4 . a. Babies have a LAD to acquire any language in the world.

b. Babies sometimes have a LAD to acquire many languages.

c. Babies have a LAD, and children acquire many languages.

5 . a. Japanese students tend to make mistakes in pronouncing the word 'often.'

b. Students in the U.S. tend to pronounce [d] for the letter t in 'better' because of their accent.

c. We sometimes have difficulties learning foreign languages because of first language interference.

4 Reading Activities 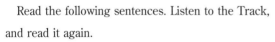 Track 2-2 ▶

Read the following sentences. Listen to the Track, and read it again.

Language Acquisition and Language Learning

Newborn babies cannot speak a language. They need about one year to start speaking a word. While they live and spend time with their caretakers, they start to acquire their first language or mother tongue. Sometimes they use another language in their com-

| newborn babies 新生児 |
| caretaker 保護者 |
| mother tongue 母語 |

dialect 方言
official language 公用語

hypothesis 仮説
a biologically specified period 生物学的に特定されたある時期
critical period 臨界期
LAD 言語習得装置
acquire 獲得する

exposure 浸す

provided with good with circumstances 良い環境が与えられれば
first-language interference 第一言語の干渉
target language 習得を目指す言語

munity. In India, for example, there are varieties of languages or dialects, so they choose English as their official language to communicate with each other. In this case, English is the second language for those children.

There is a hypothesis that babies can learn languages within a biologically specified period, which is called the critical period or sensitive period. After this period, it is difficult for babies to learn languages to the same level as native speakers.

Babies seem to be born with a LAD (language acquisition device), which allows them to learn any language on earth. Interestingly, babies can acquire more than one language if they grow up with a lot of exposure to that language. Any child can be bilingual or multilingual, if provided with good circumstances for language learning.

When we learn a second language or a foreign language, we have first-language interference. We speak the target language with our first language accent or use grammar in a non-native way. Japanese students, for example, tend to make mistakes in putting vowel sounds between or after English consonants : 'kyats' for 'cat' or 'sutoroberi' for 'strawberry', etc. Equipped with the knowlege about SLA second language acquisition (SLA), language teachers can teach the target language more effectively.

5 Mini Lectures

1 言語の習得

お母さんの声を聞いて

　赤ちゃんは，お母さんのおなかの中にいる時から周囲の音が聞こえていることが分かっています。母体を通して母親の声を聞く機会が多く，女性の声の周波数に慣れているので，生まれてきてからも女性の声に対する反応が良いということもうなずけます。男性の声の周波数は聴き慣れていないので，警戒してしまうのかもしれません。ただし，周囲の人の話し声が聞こえているからと言って，おなかの中にいる時から言語を習得しているわけではありません。話される言語の周波数や音声的特徴に慣れるようなことはあっても，語句や文構造を身につけるようなことは起こりません。妊娠中にお母さんが英語の歌やナーサリーライムを聞いたとしても，言葉の習得においてそれほどの効果は期待できないでしょう。英語が苦手なお母さんであれば，ストレスとなり，母体にもおなかの中の赤ちゃんにも好ましいとは言えないようです。

言語習得のステージ

　生後しばらくの間，9〜10か月ぐらいまでは，聴くことが中心の言語習得の期間となります。ただし，まだ何も話さないとしても言語を習得していない，あるいは，理解していないというわけではありません。話しかけられたことに対して，語・句や文を用いて反応することはなくても，表情や動きでコミュニケーションを取ることは起こっています。周囲の人の話しかけを聞き，その言葉のイントネーションをそのまま真似をして，cooing（喃語）で反応することから始めていると言われています。その後，しばらくすると，唇から息が出る時に［p］［m］［b］に近い音声が作られるようになります。保護者には「papa」や「mama」のように聞こえ，自分のことを呼んでいると嬉しくなるかもしれませんが，実際は，たまたま出た音声でしかないのかもしれません。この頃から，周囲の人の反応や話しかけを受け取る機会が増えるようになるはずです。

　次に，伝えたい内容を一語で表して表現する段階に入ります。one-word stageと呼ばれます。その後，二語を使うようになる two-words stage に，さらに，

電報文のような言葉を使うようになる telegraphic stage を経て，多くの言語使用の機会や学習を得ながら，日常生活に必要となる言葉が完成されていくことになるのです。

言語習得装置

　赤ちゃんは周囲の人が話す言語を聞くことから言語習得を始めます。周りの人が何語を話すかで母語が決まることになります。周囲の人の語りかけや関わりを通して，言語の音声的な特徴や相手の顔の表情，ジェスチャー等に触れながら言語習得がなされるわけです。保護者がたくさん話しかけて関わってあげることが大切になります。

　赤ちゃんは，何語にも対応できる言語習得装置（LAD）を持って生まれてくるので，どの言語でも短期間のうちに習得することができるのです。ただし，残念なことに，この装置は，ある時期（臨界期／critical period，敏感期／sensitive period）を過ぎると機能が失われ，いろいろな言語を習得することは難しくなってしまいます。特に，母語／第一言語を習得してしまった後では，母語習得と同じプロセスで別の言語（第二言語，外国語）を母語と同じレベルまで習得することは難しいと考えられています。

母語の干渉

　第二言語や外国語を習得する際，最初に習得した母語／第一言語の影響（母語の干渉）を受けることになります。私たちが英語を使用する際，母語の音韻構造や文構造，文法規則を当てはめて使用してしまうことで間違いが生じるのはそのためです。特に発音に関しては，その影響を受けやすく，日本語なまりの英語になってしまうのは当然のことだと考えられます。語句や文法規則においても，外来語をそのまま使用したり（part time job／アルバイト，bread／パン，sticker／シール，等），日本語の訳語をそのまま英語に置き換えたりしてしまう間違い（薬を飲む：正 take a medicine／誤 drink a medicine，絵を描く：正 draw a picture／誤 write a picture，背の高いバスケット選手：正 a tall basketball player／誤 a high basketball player，等）も同様の理由から起こっていることです。第二言語や外

国語の習得，あるいはその指導においては，学習開始年齢やどのような学習環境かが，習得のスピードや到達する言語能力への大きな要因となるようです。

2．言葉の習得で大切なこと

「刈り込み」と「関わり」の大切さ

　赤ちゃんは，生後8か月くらいまでは全ての言語音を聞き分ける能力を持っていると言われています。ただし，母語となる言語の音声や音韻体系を身につけてしまうと，他の言語の音声の習得に対しての能力は失われることになります。日本語を母語とする赤ちゃんであれば，日本語では重要でない［l］と［r］の区別ができなくなるのもその一つです。母語を習得し使用するために必要な能力だけを保ち，必要でない能力が失われる「刈り込み」が行われ，持っていた全ての言語音を聴き分けられる能力は失われることになるのです。

　赤ちゃんの言語習得について，次のような興味深い研究が行われました。生後9か月になる赤ちゃんに中国語の絵本の読み聞かせを対面で行った場合とテレビの画面を通して行った場合で，赤ちゃんの中国語の音声への反応がどのように変わるかというものです。12回の実施の後に分かったことは，対面で実施した方が，中国語の音声聞き分けの能力が優位的に高かったと言うことでした。言語の習得に関して，直接人と関わりながら言語に触れることには意味がありそうです。

言語使用を通した自動化

　語句や文構造の習得には，実際に言語を使用する機会を持つことが重要になります。その際，理解可能なインプットを多く持つことが必要になります。周囲の人との対話を通して，言葉の音声的な特徴や意味，話し手の表情や状況が脳のメモリーに蓄積されます。そして，別の機会に，同じような場面や状況において，蓄積されたデータを照合し，発信のために必要な言語形式を引き出し，音声化し伝えることが行われます。この作業を繰り返し行うことで，対応処理に必要な時間が短くなり，自動的に対応することが可能となってくるのです。当然，聴き間違いや言い間違いも起こるはずですが，周囲の人が汲み取ってく

れたり，言い直して発話してくれたりすることもあるので，その都度，データはアップデートされ，徐々に大人が持つ言語の形式に近づいていくことになります。このように，言語習得においては，最初から正しい言語形式を習得するわけではなく，時間をかけて正しい言語形式を身につけるようになるのです。言葉は使用しながら次第に洗練されていくものです。小学生の頃の話し方や書き方を大人になって続けている人はいないでしょう。時間をかけて，言語に磨きをかけ続けることで言葉が洗練されていくのです。外国語の学習においても同様だと言えるでしょう。

規則を見つけ無限の文をつくりだす

　多くのことについて理解したり発信したりできるようになるには，多くの語・句や文を使えるようになる必要があります。ただし，我々が言語を用いる際，記憶していた文をそのまま発話しているわけではありません。文を作り出すための規則が身につくと，語・句を並べかえたり，文をつなぐ方法を工夫したりすることで，様々な内容について無限に表現することができるようになります。つまり，音声，意味，語，句，文，文と文のつながりに関する様々な規則を身につけることが言語を習得することだと言えそうです。そして，その規則を知るだけでは十分ではなく，目的，場面，状況に応じて適切に使えるようになることが必要となるのです。

　子どもが「青」「青い」，「赤」「赤い」などを知ることから「緑」「緑い」という規則を作り出すことがあります。正しくはありませんが，規則の存在にきづいている，つまり，言語の習得が進んでいるということが分かります。この段階の言語能力を「中間言語（interlanguage）」と呼びます。インプット活動やアウトプット活動を通して，必要な規則を身につけること（intake）が起こっている段階にあると考えられます。この「中間言語」が生まれる豊富な言語活動を通して言語の習得が進むことになるわけです。子どもたちに自分たちの想いや考えを伝え合う豊富な言語活動の機会を持たせることで，時間をかけてインテイクが生まれ，習得が進められるようにしたいものです。

3. 第二言語の習得と外国語の学習

ESL と EFL

　生後，最初に身につける言語を母語，あるいは第一言語と言います。大抵の場合，保護者が用いる言語が第一言語として習得されることになりますが，家庭内で用いられる言語と住んでいる地域・コミュニティにおいて使用される言語が異なる場合，生活をスムーズに行うためにその言語も習得することが求められ，第二言語として習得をし，バイリンガルが生まれることになります。

　例えば，シンガポールは，中国系，インド系，イスラム系，その他のバックグラウンドが異なる人達で構成されている国ですが，英語と中国語が公用語として使用されています。ただし，家庭では，それぞれの母語が使われる場合が多いようです。学校における教育言語としては，英語が用いられる傾向になってきており，英語が公用語として使用されることが多くなってきているようです。そのような中，母語の干渉や文化的な影響が言語に影響することから，シンガポール特有の特徴のある英語が生まれることになり，「Singlish」と呼ばれるようになっています。第二言語として英語を用いているところとしては，フィリピンやインドもあげられます。

英語に触れる時間を如何に増やすことができるかが鍵

　普段のコミュニケーションにおいて自然に言語を習得する場合と教室で意識的に学習する場合では，そのプロセスに大きな違いがあります。EFL の環境にある日本やタイ，中国，韓国では，英語は普段の生活で使用される言語ではありません。学校教育を通して学ぶ対象でしかありません。小学校，中学校，高等学校の授業時数だけでは，母語話者や ESL 話者が英語に触れる時間には到底足りません。如何に授業以外の時間に英語と触れる機会を増やすかが鍵になるわけです。GIGA スクール構想が進められる中，一人一台端末の環境が整い始めています。ICT（Information and Communication Technology）を効果的に利用して英語に触れる時間を増やす工夫をすることが肝心です。また，オンラインを利用して世界の人々とつながり，実際のコミュニケーションのツールとして英語を用い Authentic な英語に触れることが英語学習の動機づけにもつなが

ります。

英語を学ぶ動機づけ

　生活のために英語を使用する ESL の場合とそうでない EFL の場合では，言語を身につける目的が異なります。ESL では，普段の会話や仕事上において，聞く，話す，読む，書く，すべての技能において，生活等に支障をきたすようなことがないレベルまで運用能力の習得が求められます。進学や就職においても，4 スキルの十分な能力が必要になります。語彙を例にとってみても，生活に用いられる基本的な語彙から，学習言語として必要になるアカデミックなものまで，また，仕事で用いる専門用語までもが必要になるわけです。一方，EFLの場合，目標となる具体的な英語力や運用能力のレベルが定まらない為，身につけなければならないという強い動機づけを得ることが難しくなってしまいます。そのため，学校の成績やテストの点数を取ることが動機づけになってしまいがちです。

　テクノロジーの進歩に伴って世界中の人達と音声や映像を同時に共有できるようになりました。オンライン上において，即興で話をしたり，テキストを送り合ったりすることが当たり前の時代です。これまでは，その場で内容を理解して返事をすることが求められたり，瞬時にメールを送り返したりするようなことがあまり求められなかったため，英語の運用能力育成に重点が置かれてこなかったのかもしれません。英語という言語に関する知識や英語圏の文化を知ることが英語教育の中心になってしまっていました。英語を学ぶ強い動機づけが不足している点が課題であったと言えるでしょう。

EFL の教育で留意すべきこと

　日本における英語教育においては，英語運用面の能力を身につけるための動機づけに留意し，英語の知識面だけの学習で終わらせることがないように注意するとともに，世界における英語という言語の役割を意識させ，いろいろな国の人たちとのコミュニケーションを可能とする国際補助言語としての英語教育の在り方が求められます。

　授業においては，目的，場面，状況を意識しながら，学習者に，どのような
コミュニケーションにしたいのかを考えさせ，実際に英語を用いて，何らかの
目的を達成したり課題を解決したりするための機会とすることが大切になりま
す。そのような学習活動を通して，英語と言う言語，その背景にある文化，コ
ミュニケーションの意義や大切さに触れることができる教育実践が期待されま
す。

6　Summary & Reflection

A　Summary

Here is a brief summary of the readings. Fill in the blanks to check your
comprehension.

It takes about one year for newborn babies to start speaking. They start with
just one word. With a lot of exposure of their caretakers' speech, babies acquire their [1](　　　) naturally. Babies can learn languages within a biologically specified period which is called [2](　　　) or sensitive period. After
this period, it is difficult for babies to learn a language at the same level as native speakers.

Babies are born with a [3](　　　) and they can learn any language easily.
Any child can be [4](　　　), or multilingual, if provided with good circumstances for language learning. In bilingual environments, they may use another
language in their community. When we learn a [5](　　　) or a foreign language, we have first language [6](　　　). Japanese students tend to make
mistakes in putting vowel sounds between or after English consonants. Language teachers are better equipped to teach the target language with the
knowledge of second language [7](　　　).

B　Reflection

　本章では，言語習得（第一言語，第二言語，外国語）について学んできました。

言語習得に関する以下の語句について，具体的な例をあげながら説明してみましょう。

	語　句	説　明
1	Babbling Stage バブリングステージ One-word Stage 一語文ステージ Telegraphic Stage 電報文ステージ	
2	Language Acquisition Device：LAD 言語習得装置	
3	Critical Period 臨界期 Sensitive Period 敏感期	
4	First Language Interference 母語の干渉	
5	Bilingual / Immersion Education バイリンガル／ イマージョン教育	

Unit 3
Vocabulary Building

1 Warm-up Activities

[A] Choose the correct meaning for the following words or phrases using (1) to (10) below.

(   ) power   (   ) sense   (   ) stationery   (   ) measure

(   ) decide   (   ) familiar   (   ) aspect   (   ) vocabulary

(   ) useful   (   ) increase

---

1 . to make a choice or judgment about something：決める

2 . things that you use for writing, such as paper, pencils, or rulers：文房具

3 . one part of an idea or something that has many parts：側面

4 . the ability or right to control people or events：権力・支配力

5 . all the words that someone knows or uses：語彙

6 . the meaning of a word, sentence, etc.：意味

7 . become bigger in amount：増加する

8 . to find the size, length, or amount of something：測る

9 . have a good knowledge or understanding of something：よく知っている

10. helps you to do something or get something you want：便利な

[B] Read the following sentences, and check the box in front of each sentence that describes you.

☐ 1 . I am a fast learner of new Japanese words that are being used these days.

☐ 2 . I like to analyze how English words are formed (e.g., 'un-'in unhappy means 'not'. So unhappy means not happy.)

☐ 3 . When I study English words, I write them down in my notebook many times.

□ 4 . I have my own special way of remembering English words.

□ 5 . I am not good at remembering English vocabulary, but when it comes to slang, I am a quick learner.

2 Aural & Oral Activities

[A] Read the questions below. Then listen to Track 3-1 and decide whether each sentence is True (T) or False (F) according to the conversation.

1 . Steve wants to be an elementary school teacher. T/F

2 . Steve answered all the quizzes correctly. T/F

3 . Steve knew what 'ruler' meant, but his answer was different from the meaning used in the textbook. T/F

4 . In last week's 'English Gaisetsu' class, both Rie and Steve learned about different aspects of vocabulary knowledge. T/F

5 . Steve feels the need to study different aspects of vocabulary. T/F

[B] Listen again and fill in the blanks.　　　　🎧**Track 3-1** ▶

Steve : I'm reading an elementary school English

　　　　textbook for a school project.

Rie :　I know you want to be an elementary school teacher.

Steve : Look, here is a word list with pictures.

Rie :　Hey, let's do a quiz! I'll read out some English words, so try to say their meanings in Japanese.

Steve :¹(　　　　　　) fun! I'm sure it will be easy for me.

Rie :　Q1 'parfait', Q2 'ruler', Q3 'play tag'.

Steve : 'Parfait' is something you eat for dessert. 'Ruler' is someone who has ²(　　　　　).

Rie :　I'm afraid ruler isn't used in that ³(　　　　　　). It is stationery used to measure things. The meaning of words ⁴(　　　　　) on what we're talking about.

Steve : Oh, I forgot it was a word from an elementary school textbook. What
⁵(   ) 'play tag'?

Rie :   It means to play '*Onigokko*'. These words are ⁶(   ) for children
to talk about themselves.

Steve : But university students like us are not ⁷(   ) with them.

Rie :   From the point of view of vocabulary knowledge, how often a word is
used or in what situations it can be used are different aspects of vocabulary knowledge. We learned that in last week's class. Do you remember?

Steve : Of course. To be a great teacher, it is not enough just to ⁸(   )
the number of words I know. I'm going to start studying different aspects of vocabulary, too!

[C] Let's try 'Role-Play Shadowing'.

1 . Listen to the Track and check the pronunciation and meaning of each word
and sentence.

2 . Try 'Role-Play Shadowing' using the Track with a partner.

3 . Change roles and repeat.

4 . Now role-play with a partner without the Track. Be sure to focus on using
the appropriate intonation, rate of utterance, and tone of voice.

[D] Talk with a partner, and take turns asking and answering the following
questions. Then, change partners, and ask and repeat.

1 . Do you like to memorize English words?

2 . How were you taught English vocabulary at school?

3 . Do you know a good way to remember English vocabulary?

4 . When you look up English words in a dictionary, what kind of information
other than the meaning do you look up?

5 . What English words do you think are useful for elementary school students

to know for self-expression activities?

3 Reading Part

A Vocabulary and Phrases

① compound word 複合語　② aspect 側面　③ depth 深さ

④ involve 含む　⑤ word formation 語形成　⑥ function 機能

⑦ uncountable noun 可算名詞　⑧ frequency 頻度　⑨ receptive 受容の

⑩ productive 発信の・発表の　⑪ cognitively 認知的に

⑫ emotionally 情意的に　⑬ demanding 負荷が高い

B True or False Questions

Read the following statements. After you have read the passage below, answer whether the sentences are True (T) or False (F) according to the passage.

1. Vocabulary is a set of meanings which only include words. T/F

2. Knowing a word in detail from different aspects is important. T/F

3. If you can use the word in speaking or writing, it can be called receptive vocabulary. T/F

4. Having a vocabulary network already formed in your native language makes it difficult to learn a second language. T/F

5. Teachers can have students memorize words by having them repeat the word one time after the teacher. T/F

C Multiple Choice

After you have read the passage below, circle the correct statements in each group.

1. a. Knowing a large amount of vocabulary and knowing a vocabulary word in depth are both important.

  b. Knowing a large amount of vocabulary is more important than knowing a vocabulary word in depth.

c. Knowing a vocabulary word in depth is more important than knowing a lot of vocabulary.

2. a. If you know that the spoken form of 'homework' is /hóumw`ək/, you have some knowledge of the word's meaning.

b. If you know that the spoken form of 'homework' is /hóumw`ək/, you have some knowledge of the word's form.

c. If you know that the spoken form of 'homework' is /hóumw`ək/, you have some knowledge of the word's usage.

3. a. Knowledge of word forms includes knowledge of how to memorize words.

b. Knowledge of word forms includes knowledge of vocabulary depth.

c. Knowledge of word forms includes knowledge of written, spoken, and word formation.

4. a. A collocation is how often the word is used.

b. A collocation is a combination of words that are often used together.

c. A collocation is the knowledge of a word you can hear or read.

5. a. It is difficult to increase second language vocabulary while keeping your native language network.

b. It is difficult to increase second language vocabulary while reforming your native language network.

c. It is difficult to increase second language vocabulary while losing your native language network.

4 Reading Activities

Track 3-2 ▶

Read the following sentences. Listen to the Track, and read it again.

Knowing a Word

compound word 複合語

A vocabulary word is a set of meanings including words, compound words, and idioms, etc. Knowing a lot of vocabulary is important in learning English. However, it is equally important to know a word in detail from many different aspects, or vocabulary depth.

aspect 側面

depth 深さ

involve 含む

Let's take a word 'homework' as an example and examine some aspects involved in knowing this word. First, there is knowledge of its word forms such as

(a) I know that the written form is 'homework'.

(b) I know that the spoken form is /ˈhóʊmwˈɚk'/.

(c) I know that this word was originally two separate words, home and work (knowledge of word formation).

word formation 語形成

Then there is knowledge of meaning, i.e., I know it means *'shukudai'* in Japanese.

function 機能

uncountable noun 不可算名詞

frequency 頻度

receptive 受容の

productive 発信の・発表の

Furthermore, there are some aspects you need to know when using the word. Those include grammatical functions (e.g., uncountable nouns), collocations (e.g., words often used with 'do'), register (e.g., words used more often in speaking than writing), and its frequency. Other aspects include whether the vocabulary knowledge is receptive (e.g., I can understand the word in listening or reading) or productive (e.g., I can use the word in speaking or writing).

One of the difficulties in learning a second language

is that your vocabulary network has already been formed in your native language. The process of increasing second language vocabulary knowledge while keeping the vocabulary network of your native language is not simple. Therefore, what can teachers do to support students?

One way is to create opportunities for students to meet a word in context repeatedly. This can increase the chances of students learning the word. In addition, teachers should teach vocabulary in a cognitively and emotionally demanding way for the students.

cognitively　認知的に

emotionally　情意的に

demanding　負荷のかかる

5　Mini Lectures

1. 語形成

語形成のプロセス

　言語は，変化しています。昔に好んで使われた言葉が「死語」として，限定的な場面でしか使われなくなったり，まったく使われなくなったりすることがあります。反対に，毎年多くの新語が生まれています。語形成（word formation）とは，新しい語が作られる際にたどったプロセスのことを指します。例えば，最近耳にする「ワンチャン」という語は，「もしかしたら」という副詞的な意味を持って使われることが多いようです。この語が形成されたプロセスを分析すると，もともと別の語として用いられていた one（形容詞）と chance（名詞）が複合名詞化し（ワンチャンス），その後，「ス」が省略されています。さらには，品詞の転換により副詞化して用いられています。本レクチャーでは，語形成の代表的なプロセスを事例と共に見ていきます。

屈折と派生

　屈折と派生は，それだけでは単語として成立しない部分（拘束形態素）を単

表 3-1　care の屈折形と派生形の例

care（動詞：気にする）	
cares（3 単現の s） cared（過去形，過去分詞形） caring（現在分詞形）	careful（注意深い） carefree（心配のない） carer（介護者）

出所：筆者作成。

語と組み合わせることで語を作ったり変化させたりするプロセスです。

　表 3-1 の左の語を見てみましょう。いずれも care という語の語尾に，拘束形態素が付加されていますが，付加される部分の性質が右枠の語とは異なります。左枠の 3 語には屈折接辞が付加されています。それぞれ異なる語形をしていますが，品詞は変わらず，辞書等では，同じ語として扱われます。動詞の 3 人称単数現在形，現在分詞形，過去形，過去分詞形，名詞の複数形，形容詞の比較級，最上級などが屈折です。一方，右枠の語は，派生接辞が付加され，品詞の異なる別語が形成されています。例えば，care(気にする)に派生接辞「-free」（〜のない）がついて carefree（心配のない・のんきな）という care とは別語ができます。ここで問題です。「fat-free」の日本語訳を答えましょう。（答え：脂肪＋〜のない→無脂肪の）このように，基本的な接辞の知識を備えていると，未知語を推測したり，学習したりする際に役に立ちます。

複合，混成，省略，転換，借用

　続いて，「複合」は，それ自体が独立して辞書に掲載されている複数の語が組み合わさって新たな語が作られるプロセスのことを指します。例えば，black（黒い：形容詞）と board（板：名詞）という語が複合されることで blackboard（黒板）ができるということです。複合の綴り方には，blackboard のように 1 語として記されるもの，high school のように，間にスペースが入るもの，well-being のように間にハイフンが入るものの三つのパターンがあります。その複合語が普及，定着するに従い，徐々に間にあったスペースやハイフンがなくなっていくようです。

　「混成」も，複数の語を組み合わせて新語を作るプロセスです。ただし，単

語と単語をそのまま組み合わせる複合とは異なり，単語の中の一部分のみを取り出して組み合わせるのが「混成」の特色です。例えば brunch という語は，breakfast と lunch の下線部を組み合わせてできた語です。類似した例には，smog（スモッグ：smoke［煙］＋fog［霧］）や，emoticon（絵文字：emotion［感情］＋icon［アイコン］）などがあります。

　多数の音節から成る語の一部を省略して短くすることで新たな語を生成するプロセスのことを「省略」と言います。語により，省略される部分は様々です。例えば，前部を残し，後部を省略するもの（例：information→ info），後部を残し，前部を省略するもの（例：telephone→ phone），そして，中央部を残し，前後を省略するもの（例：influenza→ flu）などがあります。

　語の形は変えずに品詞だけを変化させるプロセスを「転換」といいます。例えば，もともと名詞で用いられていた email という語は，現在では動詞としても使われています。同様に google という検索サイトを示す名詞は，2000年から，「(google 検索サイトを用いて) 検索する」という動詞としても使われるようになりました（Merriam-Webster dictionary）。

　他の言語からある語を借りて取り入れることを「借用」といいます。英語には様々な言語からの借用がたくさんあります。sushi や karaoke, tsunami などは，日本語からの借用です。ちなみに，オックスフォード大学出版による2015年の新語には日本語からの借用「emoji」が選ばれました。

2.　語彙指導に関わる基本概念
語彙指導の重要性

　コミュニケーション能力の育成を重視する英語教育の進展に伴い，語彙学習の重要性が高まっています。現在の学習指導要領（平成29 (2017)・30 (2018) 年告示）では中高の外国語において，学習すべき語数が増加しました。小学校においては，高学年に外国語が新設され，学習すべき語数が示されました（表3-2）。

　ここでは，小学校における語彙指導を考える際に関係する基本的な概念について説明します。

表 3-2　学習すべき語数の変化

学校種	小学校	中学校	高等学校
旧課程	―	1200	1800
新課程	600〜700	1600〜1800	1800〜2500

出所：中央教育審議会（2016）をもとに筆者作成。

語彙

　語彙とは，単語，複合語，慣用表現などから構成される意味の集合体のことです。つまり，語彙には，hand のような単語に加え，second-hand（複合語）on the other hand（慣用表現）なども含まれます。学習指導要領では，小学校において学習すべき語彙として，600〜700語程度の単語，活用頻度の高い連語（get up など）や慣用表現（excuse me など）等が示されています。

語彙知識の側面

　ある語を「知っている」と言えるのはどんな時でしょう。「その語の意味を説明できること」と考える人が多いかもしれません。意味理解は語彙知識の重要な側面の一つですが，辞書を調べると，他にも多くの側面があることに気づかされます。

　例えば，その語の発音記号，語形成，品詞，文中での働きや，その語を含んだ慣用表現，その語がどんな語と共によく使われるか（コロケーション）や頻度（どのくらい頻繁に使われるか）などが示されています。また，その語の使われる地域，媒体（文語か口語かなど），話題（日常会話か専門用語かなど）などその語が使われる範囲の制約（使用域：register）を示すものや，その語に関わる文化的知識を説明するものもあります。このように，語彙知識には多様な側面があります。普段使っている言葉にも知らない側面があるように，外国語学習においても，ある語の全ての側面を知る必要はありません。しかし，指導者が，語彙の多様な側面の知識を備えることは，より豊かな語彙指導を行う上で助けになります。

　ところで，ある語のいくつかの側面を知っていたはずなのに，いざ話そうとしたときに口から出なかったという経験をお持ちの方はいませんか。語彙知識

には受容的な側面と発信的な側面があります。受容語彙は，その語形や意味を聞いたり読んだりしたときに理解できるもの，発信語彙は，話したり書いたりして表現できる語彙を指します。英語の導入期である小学校段階では，「聞いて意味を理解できるようにする語彙と，話して表現できるようにする語彙が中心（学習指導要領解説）」になります。一般的に，語彙知識は，受容語彙から学習等を通じ徐々に発信語彙へと発展していく連続体のような状態にあると考えられています。学習指導要領では，小学校で指導する語数（600〜700語）について「発信語彙と受容語彙の両方を含めた語彙サイズであり，これらの全てを覚えて使いこなさなければならない，ということではない」と説明しています。なお，この語数は上限ではなく，児童の伝えたい内容などに応じて扱う語は追加できます。指導を計画する際には，扱う語を学習者がどのような場面で使用するか判断し，その目的に沿った指導計画が必要になります。会話の中で聞き取れればよいのか（受容語彙），それとも話せることを目指すのか（発信語彙）を判断し，適切な指導法を検討します。使用頻度や，児童の習熟度，興味・関心等も留意しましょう。

小学校で学ぶ語彙

　小学校学習指導要領「外国語科」解説では，高学年において指導する語数について「小学校段階で求められる定型の挨拶や，自分や身の回りの物事に関する簡単な描写や質問と応答，自分の考えや気持ちを述べる最も基礎的な言い回しなどに必要な語数を踏まえて設定」したと説明しています。

　小学校の検定教科書には，教科名，教室名，食べ物，動物など児童の日常生活に関わる語が多く取り上げられています。しかし，小学生にとっては身近であっても一般的な言語使用では頻度が低いものや，大学生にとってはなじみの薄いものがあります。また，音声中心で導入されたら推測できるけれど，綴りからは判別しづらい語もあり，注意が必要になります。

3. 語彙習得のプロセス

母語の場合

　Aitchison（2012）は，母語の語彙習得プロセスを三つの段階に分けて説明しています。この三段階のプロセスを「cat」を例にとり考えてみましょう。初めの段階はラベルづけです。この段階において，子どもは，ある音の連続体が，ある物を指すことに気づきます。例えば，cat という音と，お散歩中に見かけるニャーと鳴く 4 本足の動物を結びつける段階です。この段階では，まだ正確な結びつけが行われているかは分かりません。もしかしたら，4 本足の動物全てを「cat」と認識しているかもしれません。しかし，繰り返し異なる文脈でその語と出会う中で，ワンと鳴く動物は「cat」ではないこと，T シャツに描かれたニャーと鳴かない動物も「cat」と呼ばれることなどと，知識を深めていきます。このように，複数のラベルづけされた物をカテゴリーごとに整理する段階をパッケージング（箱詰め）と言います。最後の段階は，ネットワーク構築です。ここでは，全てのラベルづけされた物や，箱詰めされた概念を文脈から切り離し，言葉同士の関係を整理します。例えば，cat は，animal という言葉でも説明できるということ，さらには，より細かく種類ごとに説明できること（persian や scottishfold など），また，cat は，feed や scratch などの語と共に使われることが多いことなどの単語同士の関係性を理解し，語のネットワークを広げていきます。

　私たちは，日常生活を送る中で，日々，多くの語に出会います。初めて出会う語もありますが，普段使っている語の中の未知の側面を知ることもあります。つまり，このネットワーク構築のプロセスは，生涯にわたり継続すると考えられます。

第二言語の場合

　第二言語の場合，語彙はどのように習得されるのでしょう。まずその語に出会います。その語形を耳にするかもしれませんし，文中で出会うかもしれません。その後，その語形や意味を理解したり，様々な語彙学習ストラテジーなどを活用しながら学習したりするうちに徐々に，使えるようになります。しかし，

　第二言語の語彙習得では，既に母語での語彙ネットワークが形成されている点に注意が必要です。これは，第二言語を学習するうえでの助けとなったり，干渉を引き起こしたりします。

　日本語話者が英語の語彙を学習する際，助けとなるものに，カタカナ語があります。星野・清水（2019）は，平成29（2017）年に告示された学習指導要領に対応して作成された小学校外国語教材（『We Can!』など）にカタカナ語が含まれている割合を調査しました。結果，「高頻度で出現する英単語は日本語の中でカタカナ語として使用されているものも多く，使用されている意味も6割以上の確率でカタカナ語の意味がそのまま当てはまる」と説明しています。つまり，外国語教材に出現する英語の多くは，カタカナ語の知識を活用すれば，意味を推測できる可能性があります。

　一方，注意すべき点もあります。星野・清水（2019）の研究は，教材に出現したカタカナ語の約6割が日本語で用いられる意味で使用されていたと報告していますが，言い換えると，4割程度は，日本語として一般的に用いられる意味とは異なる意味で使われていたと言えます。論文内では，watch という語がカタカナ語辞典に掲載されている「腕時計」の意味ではなく，教材内では，「見る」という動詞として出現することが多いという例が挙げられています。

　意味以外にも，カタカナ語と本来語の間には，発音やアクセントの位置などに違いがある場合があります。これらの違いは，語彙学習を阻む要因にもなります。

　母語の語彙ネットワークを保ちながら，外国語の語彙知識を増やすプロセスは決して単純なものではありません。外国語と母語とで同じ意味を持つように思われる語であっても，意味の区切り方や範囲が異なる（例：虹と rainbow では含まれる色が違う）など，完全に一対一の対応をすることは限定的です。これらを踏まえ，第二言語の語彙習得を進めるには，その語に出会う機会を繰り返し設けましょう。指導者としては，児童の既習語を把握し，授業の単元の目標などに沿って繰り返し活用できる機会を設けましょう。既習語と新出語を意味マップ（図3-1）に整理してもよいでしょう。

　児童に語彙が表す意味をイメージさせたり，カタカナ語などの既知の知識と

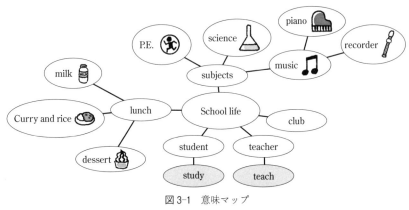

図3-1 意味マップ

出所：筆者作成。

関連づけさせたり，自己表現活動の中で用いたりさせる箇所は，認知的，情意的負荷がかかることになりますが，その分，語彙の定着を促す可能性が高くなります。

6 Summary & Reflection

A Summary

Here is a brief summary of the reading part. Fill in the blanks to check your comprehension.

Vocabulary knowledge has many [1](   ). For example, there is knowledge of word forms, their meanings, and their [2](   ). Even words we use in our [3](   ) life may have aspects that are unfamiliar to us. In foreign language learning, you do not need to know all aspects of a word. However, a teacher's knowledge of diverse aspects of vocabulary can lead to richer teaching.

[4](   ) vocabulary is words that can be heard or read. [5](   ) vocabulary is words that can be spoken or written. Many children learn English for the first time in elementary school. Thus, the focus of the lesson should be

on learning words that can be heard, and words that can be spoken.

When you plan your teaching, think about the situations in which your learners will use the word. Also [6](　　　　　　) attention to other factors. These include, for example, the frequency of the word, the child's language proficiency, and his or her [7](　　　　).

B Reflection

本章では，語形成，語彙習得及び小学校の語彙指導について学んできました。以下の語句について，具体的な例をあげながら説明してみましょう。

	語　句	説　明
1	Receptive Vocabulary 受容語彙	
2	Productive Vocabulary 発信語彙	
3	Vocabulary Depth 語彙の深さ	
4	Labelling ラベリング Packaging 箱詰め Network Building ネットワーク構築	
5	Word Formation 語形成	

Unit 4
English Sounds

1 Warm-up Activities

[A] Choose the correct meaning for the following words or phrases using (1) to (10) below.

(　　) pronounce　(　　) similarity　(　　) intelligible　(　　) feature
(　　) interference　(　　) loan word　(　　) cause　(　　) pay attention to
(　　) confusion　(　　) prosody

---

1. a characteristic or quality of someone or something：特徴

2. to make something happen：要因となる

3. the rhythm and intonation of a language：プロソディー／超分節音

4. clear enough to be understood by others：明白な，理解しやすい

5. words from one language used in another language：借用語

6. a situation in which people do not know what is happening：
   混乱している状況

7. the fact that things look or are the same：類似していること，類似点

8. to say a word：発音する，音声にする

9. to listen to someone or notice something carefully：注意を払う

10. things to prevent someone from doing something：干渉，妨害

[B] Read the following sentences, and check the box in front of each sentence that describes you.

☐ 1. I want to master native-like pronunciation of English.

☐ 2. I sometimes do not understand non-native speakers' English.

☐ 3. I believe my English pronunciation is too bad to be understood.

☐ 4. I want to use intelligible English pronunciation.

□ 5. When I talk with foreign students in Japanese, I want them to pronounce Japanese words correctly.

□ 6. We must accept some English accents because many people learn English as a foreign language.

□ 7. English teachers in elementary schools must speak English with native-like pronunciation.

2 Aural & Oral Activities

A Read the questions below. Then listen to Track 4-1 and decide whether each sentence is True (T) or False (F) according to the conversation.

1. They are talking about loan words from Chinese. T/F

2. People from other countries do not understand Japanese English at all. It sounds very different from native English. T/F

3. We need intelligible pronunciation to have good communication. T/F

4. English vowels are basically the same as Japanese ones. T/F

5. Prosody is very important only if we speak in English with non-native speakers. T/F

B Listen again and fill in the blanks.　　　　🎧Track 4-1 ▶

Rie :　Steve, will you tell me how to ¹(　　　　)
　　　 these words?

Steve : Sure. Strawberry, sandwich, badminton, and fingers.

Rie :　They sound similar in Japanese, but different.

Steve : You are right. The Japanese language has ²(　　　　) words from English. However, their pronunciations are different from English. If Japanese people use those loan words in English conversation, native speakers of English won't understand them because of their different pronunciations.

Rie :　We should learn intelligible pronunciation to communicate well with foreign people, right?

Steve : Exactly. Japanese people ³(   ) to have mother tongue interferences in English, which sometimes makes it difficult for people from other countries to understand.

Rie : What should we pay attention to when we speak in English?

Steve : Some Japanese features of pronunciation may cause confusion in conversations.

Rie : I need to know them and make my English intelligible.

Is it hard to ⁴(   ) how to pronounce English sounds well?

Steve : No, not really. First, you should know the differences between Japanese sounds and English ones.

Rie : I see. Do you mean ⁵(   ) sounds and vowel sounds?

Steve : Yes. In addition to those segmental sounds, prosody is also the key in letting your listeners understand you.

Rie : Prosody?

Steve : That means word stress, sentence stress, and intonation. Among non-native speakers or native speakers, prosody is very important to

⁶(   ) your English intelligible.

C Let's try 'Role-Play Shadowing'.

1. Listen to the Track and check the pronunciation and meaning of each word and sentence.

2. Try 'Role-Play Shadowing' using the Track with a partner.

3. Change roles and repeat.

4. Now role-play with a partner without the Track. Be sure to focus on using the appropriate intonation, rate of utterance, and tone of voice.

D Talk with a partner, and take turns asking and answering the following questions. Then, change partners, and ask and repeat.

1．Do you think your English pronunciation is intelligible?

2．Do you have any difficulties pronouncing English sounds?

3．Which do you think is more difficult, English intonation or word stress?

4．Do you know the difficulties speakers of other languages have with Japanese sounds or words?

5．What is the best way to master English pronunciation?

3　Reading Part

A　Vocabulary and Phrases

① lingua franca 共通言語　② in addition to 付け加えて　③ notice 気づく

④ difficulty 困難　⑤ the following features 次の特徴　⑥ cause 引き起こす

⑦ confusion 混乱　⑧ add 付け加える　⑨ combination 組み合わせ

⑩ improve 改善する　⑪ intelligible 明瞭な　⑫ except 〜を除けば

⑬ require 求める　⑭ position 職位　⑮ accent 発音の特徴，なまり

B　True or False Questions

Read the following statements. After you have read the passage below, answer whether the sentences are True (T) or False (F) according to the passage.

1．English is used only to talk to native speakers of English. T/F

2．The number of ESL users is more than EFL learners now. T/F

3．Talking to non-native speakers of English is easier than talking to native speakers of English on the global stage. T/F

4．Japanese tend to put unnecessary vowel sounds in English words. T/F

5．The word 'intelligible' has a similar meaning to 'intellectual'. T/F

6．Wrong pronunciation does not cause any problems in communication among non-native speakers of English. T/F

7．All learners of the English language should master native-like pronunciation. T/F

C̲ Multiple Choice

After you have read the passage below, circle the correct statements in each group.

1. a. Non-native English speakers speak English intelligibly.

   b. A non-native English speaker's first language is not intelligible.

   c. For non-native English speakers, intelligibility is also significant.

2. a. The number of EFL speakers is less than the number of ESL speakers.

   b. The number of ESL speakers is less than the number of EFL speakers.

   c. The number of native English speakers is less than the number of ESL and EFL speakers combined.

3. a. Japanese students tend to use nasalized vowels.

   b. Japanese students tend to use the wrong sounds.

   c. Japanese students tend to add many consonant sounds.

4. a. Teaching pronunciation is a key to make learners' English intelligible.

   b. Teaching pronunciation is not necessary for learners to communicate better with non-native speakers.

   c. Teaching pronunciation is very important only when learners want to be a spy in the future.

5. a. At the United Nations, people from many countries use English with British accents.

   b. At the United Nations, people from many countries are expected to speak English with an American accent.

   c. At the United Nations, people from many countries use English with their accents.

4 Reading Activities

🎧Track 4-2 ▶

Read the following sentences. Listen to the Track, and read it again.

Teaching Pronunciation

These days many people use English as an international language or a lingua franca across the globe. In addition to talking with native speakers of English, learners of English may use this language to speak to other learners of English, or non-native speakers of English, too. In fact, the number of ESL and EFL users is more than that of native English speakers now. Thus, we should also notice the difficulties in communicating with non-native speakers of English when we use English on the global stage.

Japanese students have the following features of English pronunciation, which can cause confusion in communication : (1) using the wrong sound, (2) adding vowel sounds, (3) using the wrong word stress, (4) using the wrong sentence stress, (5) using the wrong intonation pattern and (6) combinations of (1) — (5).

Teaching pronunciation is the key for English learners to improve their intelligibility. Communication may break down without intelligible pronunciation. However, we do not need the same ability as native speakers of English, unless you need it for your job interview, which requires a more advanced level of English for a position, for instance. At the United Nations, peo-

a lingua franca 共通語

ESL / EFL

English as a second Language 第二言語／ English as a foreign language 外国語として の英語

thus それ故に

features 特徴

cause 引き起こす

confusion 混乱

add つけ足す

word stress 語強勢

sentence stress 文強勢

intelligibility 明瞭性

break down 成り立たなくなる

advanced level 高度なレベル

position 職

ple worldwide work together to make a peaceful world using English in spite of their accents.

5 Mini Lectures

1. 英語と日本語の違い

英語と日本語の言語間の距離

　世界に存在する言語を統語的・意味論的特徴によって分類すると，英語は，印欧語族（Indo-European Language），西ゲルマン語派で，日本語とは異なる言語類になります。英語と日本語では言語間の距離がかなり遠いので，音声や音韻構造においても違いがあります。英語母語話者と英語で話をしようとする場合，その音声的な違いから，相手の発話が十分に理解できなかったりこちら側の英語がうまく伝わらなかったりすることが起こってしまいます。

日本語と英語の違いを意識する

　言語音には，各言語で用いられる個々の音声（分節音／segmental sounds）に加えて，強勢（stress）やイントネーション（intonation）等の語句や文全体に関わる音声的な特徴であるプロソディー／超分節音（prosody / suprasegmental sounds）があります。母語習得においては，この分節音，超分節音の両方についての知識や音を産出する能力を無意識的に習得し，身につけているのですが，外国語となると話は別です。既に，母語の音声・音韻構造を習得してしまっている段階では，意識的に学習やトレーニングを行わない限り，母語の音声との違いに気づいたり産出したりすることが難しくなります。

有声音と無声音

　言語音には，有声音と無声音があります。有声音とは，声帯が震える音声のことで，無声音は声帯が震えない音声のことです。喉仏のあたりに指先を軽く当てて発話すると，声帯が震える有声音と震えない無声音の違いを確かめることができます。[p]［t］［k］［s］［f］等は声帯が震えない無声音ですが，声帯が震えた場合は，[b]［d］［g］［z］［v］の音声になります。日本語の「あ」「い」

「う」「え」「お」の母音は声帯が震える有声音です。ささやき声で発音される場合，声帯は震えることはありません。

英語の分節音

　英語の分節音について見てみましょう。英語の音声を大きく分けると母音（vowels）と子音（consonants）に分けることができます。母音は口腔内で肺から上がってきた気流が声帯を震わせて作られた音が，舌の高さや形，唇の形や開きによって異なる特徴を持つ音声となって産出されるものです。日本語の母音は五つ："ア，イ，ウ，エ，オ"しかありませんが，英語の母音は数が多く，日本語の"ア"に聞こえる音声の特徴を持った母音が四つは少なくともあると言えそうです（/æ/ /ʌ/ /ɑ/ /ə/）。例えば，「bat」：コウモリ，「butt」：タバコ，「bot」：ハエの幼虫は，母音の発音の違いだけで別の単語として認識されるわけです。これらの日本語では区別されない音声については，特に意識しながら学ぶことが大切です。指導の際は，学習者にその違いに気づかせるために，強く長めに発音して聞かせてあげることがポイントになります。

　子音は，口腔内や唇等で何らかの妨げを受ける音声で，閉鎖音（stops）：［p］［b］［t］［d］［k］［g］，摩擦音（fricatives）：［θ］［ð］［s］［z］［ʃ］［ʒ］［f］［v］，破擦音（affricates）：［ʧ］［ʤ］，鼻音（nasals）：［n］［m］［ŋ］等があります。いずれの子音も日本語の子音を調音する時よりも呼気量を多くして，破裂や摩擦，破擦が強く起こる発音をすると英語の音声特徴に近くなるようです。

英語のプロソディー／超分節音

　伝えたい内容にあったイントネーション，語強勢，文強勢を用いて発話しないと異なった意味で伝わる可能性があります。文末が上がり調子か下がり調子かで意味が変わることは良く知られているところです。「You like natto.」を上昇調で発話すると「君は納豆が好きなの」と言う質問に聞こえます。また，「Excuse me.」を上がり調子で発話すると「もう一回言ってもらえますか」に，下がり調子で発話すると「すみません」になります。「research」は，前の音節を強く言うと名詞に，後音節を強く言うと動詞になります。「I saw a cat on the bench.」の場合，前後の文脈によっては，どの語を強く発話するかで意味も違ってきます。声の調子（Tone of voice）に話者の気持ちを表すことができることも重要なポイントと言えるでしょう。

2. 通じる発音を目指して
リンガ・フランカ・コア

　日本語の影響を強く受けた発音で英語を発音すると，伝えたい内容がうまく伝わらないことがあります。例えば，「Will you tell me the nearest McDonald around here?」は，「McDonald」のアクセントの位置を正しく第二音節に置いて発音できないとハンバーガーを食べることができなくなったりします。通じる英語にするには，どのような点を意識しておくべきか，一緒に考えてみましょう。

　英語は，世界中のいろいろな地域で外国語として学ばれているだけでなく，第二言語として用いられているところもあります。その数を合わせると，英語を母語とする人たちより多いと言われています。結果として，世界では，それぞれの母語の影響を受けた様々な英語が使われているのも事実です。

　母語が異なる人々が存在する状況において，一つの言語が共通の言語として使われる時，その言語をリンガ・フランカと呼びます。英語がリンガ・フランカとして用いられる現在の世界状況において，母語話者にも非母語話者にとってもお互いに理解しやすい発音や語句・表現の選択が期待されることになります。ある特定の文化や言語に偏らないグローバルなステージにおけるコミュニケーションのツールとして，新たな英語の姿が生まれてきていると考えて良いでしょう。

　Jenkins（2015）はリンガ・フランカとしての英語の発音に関して，共通しておさえておくべきコア（核）となるリンガ・フランカ・コア（Lingua Franca Core）のポイントを以下のようにまとめています。

　①子音の発音（ただし，th の発音や dark l の発音はのぞく）
　②母音の長さの違いによる語の区別を明確にする

　③語頭の子音は発音する

　④語中，語尾の子音は発音する

　⑤文強勢を正しい位置に置く

英語の多様性を意識した指導

　EFL の環境における英語の音声指導において，英語母語話者の発話がモデルとして録音された教材を使用することが多いようです。ただし，リンガ・フランカとして英語が用いられている事実を考えると，世界で使われる英語の多様性にふれることも大切であることが分かります。今後は，様々なバックグラウンドを持つ人たちとの英語でのコミュニケーションの機会が増えることが予測されます。その際，非母語話者が用いる英語や文化に対しての偏見や間違った先入観を与えないように留意する必要があると言えるでしょう。特に小学校段階では，「母語話者の英語のみが正しい，美しい英語である」と思わせてしまうような指導にならない配慮が求められます。言語，文化の相対性を意識しながら，様々な人々によって使用されている英語の姿をそのまま伝えることは大切だからです。

身につけるべき発音とは

　外国語として英語を学ぶ学習者の場合，発音の到達目標をどのレベルに設定するかがポイントになります。子どもの音声面への柔軟な適応力には驚くものがありますが，過度な発音の指導や発音の矯正は，子どもが英語を学ぶことへの心理的なバリアを高くするだけのようです。日本語の音声・音韻体系を既に習得している子どもたちが，初めて英語を学び始めることになるのだとすると，母語話者と同レベルの音韻認識能や発音が身につくとは考えられません。

　Zielinski（2008）は，母語話者と非母語話者間におけるコミュニケーションに支障をきたさないための明瞭性に関する研究において，英語母語話者が，話されている情報の中心となる語彙の聞き取りに利用するのは，単語の強勢パターンと強音節が置かれる分節音の音声であるとしています。また，個々の分節音の指導と強勢パターンの指導を行う際，別々に分けて指導するのではなく，

単語・句や文を発話する練習を通して，同時に行うことが望ましいとしています。その方が，音のつながりの中での音声指導になるだけではなく，発話している内容・意味を意識した発音練習が可能となるからです。

3. 音声指導のポイント

　小学校の授業を参観すると，手拍子に合わせて英文を発話させる風景を目にすることがあります。語や句，文の中での聞こえ（卓立）の高い強音節と聞こえが低い弱音節の現れによる英語の強勢パターンのリズムと音楽のリズムやテンポとを同じだと勘違いしてしまい，単に手拍子に合わせた発話活動で終わっている場合があるようです。英語のリズムを指導しているつもりなのかもしれませんが，実際には，語や句，文の中の卓立の特徴，イントネーション，音調核を意識するような提示や練習にはなっていないため，効果的な音声指導とは言えません。

　ナーサリーライム（わらべ歌）や歴代大統領スピーチ等に現れる特徴的な英語の強勢拍リズムは，まとまりのある英文において周期的に卓立の置かれる場所が現れることで聞き手に韻律的効果を感じさせることになるものです。ただし，普段の会話，特に短い対話において多く現れるものではありません。小学生が韻律を整える技法を習得する必要はないでしょうし，文化的背景を知らなければ，大人でも難解なナーサリーライムや児童の発達段階に合わない大統領スピーチ等をモデル教材として用いる必要もないはずです。

想いを表現する発話練習を通した指導から

　子どもたちにしてみれば，自分の思いや考えを発信するために英語を学んでいるわけですから，伝えたい内容が適切に相手に伝わるように，語・句・文の強勢位置を意識した発音練習を行うことが望まれるはずです。前後の音声環境における分節音のつながりの特徴や強勢パターン，イントネーションに慣れる時間を多く持つ方が自己表現につながる活動としても望ましいと言えそうです。表現したい内容，自分の想いや考え，気持ちが，相手に伝わるための発話練習を通して，結果として，英語の音声的な特徴も身につけられる指導を目指した

いものです。

今後の音声指導の方向性

　Celce-Murcia, et al.（2010）は，これからの発音指導のためのカリキュラムデザインについて述べており，授業時数，教育環境，学習者因子に応じて到達可能なレベルを設定するべきであるとし，グローバルステージにおける英語使用を想定した音声指導プログラムの必要性を説いています。

　また，Kirkpatrick（2007）は，伝統的に実施されてきた標準モデルや規範的な音声に関する知識を目標として学ぶのではなく，コミュニケーション能力の育成を目指す英語教育の視点から，リンガ・フランカ・コアとしての英語音声指導のアプローチの方が，教師にも学習者にも実現可能な到達目標を目指せる点において利点があるとしています。

　Morley（1999）は，機能的明瞭性を目指すことで，発音習得への意識を高めると同時に，状況に応じた効果的なコミュニケーション能力（communicability）の育成を目指すことが重要であると考えています。これらの考えは，これからの新たな英語音声指導の指針となりそうです。

受信レベルと発信レベルの音声指導を意識する

　音声指導について考える際，受信レベルと発信レベルの両方の視点から捉えることが重要です。ややもすると発音／発信レベルの指導になりがちですが，まずは，聴く／受信レベルの丁寧な指導から取り組む必要があります。また，ボトムアップ，トップダウンの両アプローチから音声能力を育てることが重要であり，実際の指導においては，個々の分節音の指導に加えてプロソディーの指導も重要となります。音の流れの中から語強勢や文強勢をヒントに語境界やセンスグループとして情報を聴き取る能力の育成が期待されます。その際，児童の発達段階に適した教材や指導法を選ぶことの大切さに加え，実際の指導方法や適切な教材の開発も望まれるところです。

　英語学習の入門期においてこそ音声面の指導は大切になります。小学校段階から質の良い指導や教材が提供されることが，後の英語能力につながる基礎力

育成の機会として重要な役割を果たすことが期待されるからです。ただし，無味乾燥な一つひとつの分節音の発音練習ばかりでは，言葉を学ぶ楽しさを得ることはできないはずです。小学生の発達段階や多重知性を考慮した，多様な音声指導教材が必要になるはずです。

6 Summary & Reflection

Here is a brief summary of the readings. Fill in the blanks to check your comprehension.

As an ¹(   ), people use English in many places, and we may have opportunities to communicate with people who use English as a second language or a ²(   ). The Japanese language influences English ³(   ). This influence makes it difficult to communicate well with people across the globe. We need to have the knowledge or ability to ⁴(   )well with both the native and ⁵(   ) of English. It is not easy to master native-like pronunciation, but ⁶(   ) is the key to having people understand you well. In English teaching, we should teach students intelligible pronunciation to avoid communication ⁷(   ) due to their accents. If students need an advanced level of English in the future, they may have special pronunciation lessons or take a course in English phonetics.

F Reflection

本章では，英語の音声的な特徴，日本語の音声との違いについて学んできました。英語の音声に関する以下の語句について，具体的な例をあげながら説明してみましょう。

	語　句	説　明
1	Lingua Franca 共通言語	
2	Accent 訛り	
3	Sentence Stress 文強勢	
4	Intonation イントネーション	
5	Intelligibility 明瞭性	

Unit 5
Intercultural Communication

1 Warm-up Activities

A Choose the correct meaning for the following words or phrases using (1) to (10) below.

(　　) assignment 　(　　) home economics 　(　　) analogy

(　　) similarity 　(　　) feature 　(　　) layer 　(　　) peel

(　　) end up ～ing 　(　　) unaware 　(　　) lesson

---

1. a comparison of two things that has similar points：たとえ，比喩

2. something you learn through experience：教訓

3. a word used to compare things that are alike：類似点

4. a typical or important part of something：特徴

5. to find yourself at the end of a place or situation：～してしまう

6. a school subject that usually includes the study of cooking, sewing and other skills needed at home：家庭科

7. to take off the skin from fruit or vegetables：（皮を）むく

8. a sheet of something that covers a surface or is between surfaces：層

9. not knowing what is happening：気がつかない

10. a task that a student is given to do：課題

B Read the following sentences, and check the box in front of each sentence that describes you.

☐ 1. I like to know about foreign cultures.

☐ 2. I am good at communicating in my first language.

☐ 3. The most important factor when communicating in English is to have a large amount of English vocabulary knowledge.

□ 4 . The most important factor when communicating in English is the knowledge of body language.

□ 5 . When communicating in English, factors 3 (vocabulary) and 4 (body language) above are important. However, I think there is something even
more important.

2 Aural & Oral Activities

A Read the questions below. Then listen to Track 5-1 and decide whether
each sentence is True (T) or False (F) according to the conversation.

1 . Rie is working on her assignment for home economics. T/F

2 . An onion and fish in water are analogies of culture. T/F

3 . Steve was able to peel onions well the first time he used them in cooking.
T/F

4 . Steve is shaped only by Japanese culture. T/F

5 . The fish in water analogy explains that we are not aware of the influence of
culture until we are out of it. T/F

B Listen again and fill in the blanks.　　　　🎧**Track 5-1** ▶

Rie :　Hi, Steve! I am working on my assignment for
next week's class. Can you help me?

Steve : Let me see… a picture of an onion and a fish in water. Is this an assignment for home ¹(　　　　)?

Rie :　No, it's a class on intercultural communication. These pictures are analogies of culture. We have to find ²(　　　　) between these pictures
and the ³(　　　　) of a culture.

Steve : Interesting. Let's see, onion is brown.

Rie :　Hmm… does it explain something?

Steve : An onion has many ⁴(　　　　). The first time I used onions in my
cooking, I did not know how far to peel them. I ended up ⁵(　　　　)

too much and $^6($ $)$ too little of it.

Rie :　I got the point! An onion's layer tells us that people are also shaped by many different cultures.

Steve : I understand what you mean. I am shaped by not only Japanese culture. My rock culture and cat lover culture are also a part of me.

Rie :　What about a fish in the water?

Steve : Have you ever heard the following Chinese proverb? "If you want to know what water is like, don't ask a fish in a bowl."

Rie :　I got it! We are unaware that we are $^7($ $)$ the influence of our culture. Just like this fish is unaware of water!

Steve : Yeah. But once you are out of the water of the bowl, you realize that you depend so much on it.

Rie :　Wow! That gives us a lot of $^8($ $)$ on the importance of better communication!

C　Let's try 'Role-Play Shadowing'.

1 . Listen to the Track and check the pronunciation and meaning of each word and sentence.

2 . Try 'Role-Play Shadowing' using the Track with a partner.

3 . Change roles and repeat.

4 . Now role-play with a partner without the Track. Be sure to focus on using the appropriate intonation, rate of utterance and tone of voice.

D　Talk with a partner, and take turns asking and answering the following questions. Then, change partners, and ask and repeat.

1 . Are you good at communicating with others?

2 . Are you good at communicating with others using English?

3 . What do you think is the difference between communicating in Japanese and communicating in English?

4. Have you ever used English to communicate with people from other countries outside of school?

5. What is the most important thing when you communicate using English?

3 Reading Part

A Vocabulary and Phrases

① separate 切り離す　② cultural background 文化的背景

③ competence 能力　④ describe 記述する

⑤ sociolinguistic 社会言語学に関する

⑥ pragmatic 語用論的な（文脈における言語使用）　⑦ interact 交流する

⑧ component 構成要素　⑨ attitude 態度

⑩ critical cultural awareness クリティカルな文化意識　⑪ acquire 獲得する

⑫ curiosity 好奇心　⑬ abstract 抽象的な　⑭ diverse 多様な

⑮ evolve 進化する

B True or False Questions

Read the following statements. After you have read the passage below, answer whether the sentences are True (T) or False (F) according to the passage.

1. When learning a foreign language, one cannot do without learning about the culture attached to it. T/F

2. Communicative language competences include intercultural competence or IC. T/F

3. According to Byram, there are four components of IC : attitude, knowledge, skills and awareness. T/F

4. During elementary school might be a good time for the teachers to develop their students' 'knowledge' of foreign culture. T/F

5. Students in the fifth and sixth grades gradually develop the ability to think abstractly. T/F

Multiple Choice

After you have read the passage below, circle the correct statements in each group.

1. a. One cannot learn a language without drinking alcohol.

   b. One cannot learn a language without running every morning.

   c. One cannot leave culture out of language learning.

2. a. When communicating in a foreign language, a speaker and listener's foreign language ability is the only factor that affects communication.

   b. When communicating in a foreign language, both a speaker and listener's foreign language ability and their cultural backgrounds affect communication.

   c. When communicating in a foreign language, only the speaker's foreign language ability and cultural background are important, but not those of the listener.

3. a. According to the CEFR, communicative competence is described using two components : communicative language competence and general competence.

   b. According to the CEFR, communicative competence is described using three components : linguistic competence, socio-linguistic competence and pragmatic competence.

   c. According to the CEFR, communicative competence is described using four components : attitudes, knowledge, skills and critical cultural awareness.

4. a. The concept of IC tells us that the goal of foreign language learning is to be able to pronounce a language at a native speaker level.

   b. The concept of IC tells us that our goal in learning a foreign language is not to become a native speaker.

c. The concept of IC tells us that the goal of foreign language learning is to always get high scores on a vocabulary test.

5 . a. One tip for developing ICs for 5th and 6th graders is to think of ways to let them 'experience' other people's perspectives.

b. One tip for developing ICs for 5th and 6th graders is to think of ways to make them sing English songs every day.

c. One tip for developing ICs for 5th and 6th graders is to think of ways to make them memorize cultural knowledge.

4　Reading Activities　🎧Track 5-2 ▶

Read the following sentences. Listen to the Track, and read it again.

Competence to Communicate in a Foreign Language

Learning a language and culture cannot be separated. When communicating using a foreign language, not only foreign language ability but also cultural background of the speaker and listener will affect communication. Then, which competences are needed when communicating with people who do not share a common background? The Common European Framework of Reference for Languages or CEFR（2001）describes communicative competence in two parts : communicative language competences and general competences. Communicative language competences are those which are important when communicating using language. These include linguistic competences, sociolinguistic competences and pragmatic compe-

competence 能力

describe 記述する

sociolinguistic 社会言語学に関する

63

pragmatic 語用論的

interact 交流する
components 構成要素

attitude 態度
critical cultural aware-
ness クリティカルな文化
意識

acquire 獲得する
curiosity 好奇心

abstract 抽象的な

diverse 多様な

tences. Competences which are less closely related to language are called 'general competences'. These includes knowledge of the world, study skills, and intercultural competence.

Intercultural competence or IC is an ability to interact with people from other cultures. Byram (1997) explains that the four components of IC are attitudes, knowledge, skills and critical cultural awareness. The concept of IC tells us that the goal of foreign language learning is not to become native speakers of a foreign language.

How can we develop IC in elementary school children? What can the teachers start with? Here are some tips.

· Since elementary school students are in the process of acquiring cultural knowledge, they are open minded and full of curiosity about other cultures. It might be a good time for the teachers to develop students' 'attitude' toward foreign cultures.

· In the 5th and 6th grades, students gradually develop abstract thinking. Therefore, be careful not to make the class only about learning cultural knowledge. It would be nice if you can think of ways to allow students to 'experience' others' viewpoints, such as acting them out.

As globalization progresses, the cultural backgrounds of English speakers are becoming more diverse. In addition, technologies such as machine translation are evolving dramatically. In this modern age, the importance of developing IC will grow.

5　Mini Lectures

1.　英語学習における異文化間能力育成の重要性
異文化間能力の定義

　言語の学習と文化の学びは切り離すことができません。例えば，lemon（レモン）は，その酸味から日本語ではさわやかなイメージがありますが，英語では反対に否定的なイメージがあります（欠陥品など）。このように，一つの単語の背後にも，文化の違いが存在します。英語を用いてコミュニケーションを図るとき，言葉が正確でも，うまく伝わらないことがあります。言葉に付随してあらわれるジェスチャーや表情，話者と聞き手との価値観や当然と思うことの違いなどが，意図しない誤解を招いたりします。そこには，個人のもつ文化的背景が影響しています。

　自分とは異なる文化を持つ他者と共通理解の構築を目指してコミュニケーションを行う際に必要になる能力を異文化間能力（Intercultural Competence：IC）といいます。Byram（1997）は，その構成要素として，次の四つを挙げています。

　　・態度：好奇心，開かれた心，異文化・自文化についての考えを保留できる
　　・知識：自国および交流する相手国における社会集団の産物や慣習に対する
　　　知識，交流の一般的プロセスに対する知識
　　・スキル：異文化を解釈し，自文化と関連付けるスキル，実際の交流の中で
　　　各構成要素を運用するスキル
　　・クリティカルな文化意識：明確な基準に基づきクリティカルに自文化・異
　　　文化を評価する能力

　異文化間能力の育成では，「態度」が基盤となります。特に，自文化や異文化についての知識の習得過程にある小学生は柔軟で，異文化に対する興味や好

奇心にあふれており，態度面の指導に適した時期といえます。

　グローバル化の進展に伴い，英語話者の文化的背景は多様化しています。また，機械翻訳などの技術も劇的に進化しています。このような現代において，ICの育成は，重要性を増しています。Mercer, et al.（2019）は，21世紀市民に求められるスキルの内，英語授業の中で扱うことに適しているものとしてICを挙げています。

文化とは

　本節の冒頭では，コミュニケーションに文化が多大な影響を及ぼしていることを述べました。では「文化」とは，何でしょう。文化の説明にFive Fsという表現が用いられることがあります。これは，Food, Fashion, Famous people, Festivals, and Flags（食べ物，ファッション，有名人，祭り，国旗）の略語です。しかし，このような目に見える文化（表層文化）は，文化の総体のほんの一部に過ぎません。見えているわずかな部分の下にはより大きな部分があるという点から文化は氷山に例えられます。文化の氷山モデルにおいて，海面下に潜んでいるのは，社会的規範や価値観などの目には見えない文化（深層文化）です。深層文化は，表層文化とつながっており，コミュニケーションにおいて，トラブルの種ともなります。例えば，自分が開いたホームパーティに，友人が約束の時間よりも30分早く訪れたとします。ある文化では，親しい間柄では，パーティを準備段階から手伝うと良いという考えがあります。また別の文化では，準備の邪魔をしては悪いので少し遅れて訪れるべきという考えがあります。その文化での時間の捉え方によって，同じ行動であっても，感謝されたりトラブルとなったりします。よりよいコミュニケーションのためには，表面的に現れた言動だけで他者を評価するのではなく，判断をいったん保留し，目に見える行動に影響を及ぼしている深層文化を理解しようとする姿勢を持つことが大切です。

　このようなトラブルは，同じ国であっても，地域や年代，宗教や育った家庭環境が違えば起こりえます。例えば，引っ越しや進学により，今までの常識が通用しなくなった経験がその例です。このように文化は多層的です。

　個人のアイデンティティも多層的で，多様な文化（例えば，国民文化，地域文化，若者文化など）の影響を受けています。そして，その構成要素は，様々な影響を受けて変化します。皆さんも，大学生になり，高校時代とは異なる文化を体験したり，新たに身につけたりしているのではないでしょうか。文化は，常に変化します。

2.　コミュニケーションにおいて求められる能力
コミュニケーションのプロセス

　学習指導要領で外国語教育の目標を見ると，小中高においてコミュニケーション能力の育成が掲げられています。英語の知識ではなく，英語を用いてコミュニケーションを図る能力の育成が重要であることが分かります。

　それではまず，口頭でコミュニケーションを行う際，どのような段階をたどるか考えてみます。

　話し手は，言語を通して伝えたい内容を計画し，伝えたい内容を表現するために適切な語彙を選び，文法を考慮しながら，発話します。相手に伝わりやすくするために，非言語コミュニケーションなども活用するかもしれません。では，聞き手はどうでしょう。発話された言語を受け取り，それを通じて話し手が伝えたかった内容を理解・解釈します。それを受け，聞き手は場合によっては話し手となり，聞いて理解する作業と並行して，相手との文化的差異を考慮しながら，自分が伝えたい内容やそのために必要な言語材料についての計画を進めます。これらの段階は同時並行的に起こることもあります。母語では自然に行っている一連の行動ですが，改めて考えると，非常に複雑です。

　コミュニケーションは，社会的文脈の中で生じます。そのため，同じ言語形式で同じ意味を持つ表現が使用されても，それが発される場面や状況により，伝えられるメッセージは異なります。例えば，「That's funny」が，「それ面白い！」という誉め言葉から，皮肉にもなります。さらに，発話者と聞き手の社会文化的知識が伝え方や理解する内容に影響を与えます。

　学習指導要領に影響を及ぼした文書に，欧州評議会によるヨーロッパ言語共通参照枠（CEFR, 2001）があります。この CEFR は，人の全ての能力が，言語

使用者がコミュニケーションを行う力に何らかの形で寄与するという点から，全ての能力をコミュニケーション能力の一部であると捉えています。その上で，それらを言語に直接関係するもの（コミュニケーション言語能力）と，それ以外（一般的能力）に分けて説明しています。コミュニケーション言語能力には，言語能力（語彙や文法などの言語に関わる知識と運用スキル），社会言語能力（言語使用に求められる社会的な側面。例えば，敬語の使い方や非言語コミュニケーションについての知識と運用スキルなど）と言語運用能力（ある社会文化的コンテキストで適切な言語運用ができる能力）が含まれます。一般的能力には，学習者の性格的要因や学習能力，異文化間能力などが含まれます。

　このようにコミュニケーションのプロセスは複雑で，その遂行には，言語能力に加え，様々な能力が求められます。

異文化間教育の意義

　Mini Lectures 1 では，Byram（1997）による IC の構成要素を紹介しました。ここから，他者との共通理解を深めるには，コミュニケーションを行う相手文化の歴史や，習慣などの知識を得るだけでは十分でないことが分かります。相手を肯定的に受け止めたり，相手について自文化に基づいた判断を一旦保留したりする態度が必要になります。また，コミュニケーション相手の行動に影響を及ぼしている習慣や価値観について，自文化との比較や関連付けを通して，解釈しようするスキルも求められます。その過程では，自文化中心の視点を離れ，自分や相手の文化的背景や社会的文脈を批判的相対的に捉えようとする力も必要になります。このような認識や態度を育成する教育を異文化間教育と言います。自分と他者との異なる視点を行き来することで，偏見や自文化中心主義の克服，批判的視点の獲得，そして他者への寛容性を高めることが期待されます。カルトン（2015）は，異文化間教育の意義を「他者を認め，自分の心を開き，他者の考え方に思いをめぐらせ，『自分のものの見方が唯一の見方』という思考から抜け出し，他者は異なっているとの考え方を受け入れ，その違いも正しいものと理解できる」ことと説明します。

　このような教育は，どの教科でも実践できますが，特に，異なる視点との出

会いの機会が豊富で，コミュニケーション能力の育成を目標とする外国語の授業は，大きな役割を果たします。日本と比べて言語や文化の多様性の高いヨーロッパでは，過去に行われた言語権の侵害と戦争への反省から，言語と文化の多様性を「価値ある共通の資源（Council of Europe, 2001）」と捉えています。欧州評議会の欧州現代言語センターでは，外国語教育を通じた IC 育成の重要性を理念に掲げ，これらを推進する教育政策や CEFR をはじめとする様々なツール，実践等を数多く展開しています（Unit 14）。

3．小学校の英語授業を通じた異文化間能力育成

小学校外国語科（英語）の目標と教材に見られる IC 育成の視点

　小学校外国語活動では，導入に至る経緯から，異文化理解の視点が重視されてきました。平成29（2017）年に改訂された小学校学習指導要領（外国語）においても，この視点の重要性が観察されます。例えば，第 1 　目標（3）には，「学びに向かう力，人間性等」にかかる目標として「外国語の背景にある文化に対する理解を深め，他者に配慮しながら，主体的に外国語を用いてコミュニケーションを図ろうとする態度を養う。」ことが示されています。言語に加えて相手の文化を理解しようとすること，他者に配慮したり尊重したりすることは，IC にもつながる要素と解釈できます。また，第 3 　指導計画の作成と内容の取扱い（3）「教材選定の観点」においても，（ア）「多様な考え方に対する理解を深めさせ（るもの）」や（ウ）「国際協調の精神を養うのに役立つこと」などが示されています。一方，その具体的な指導法については明記されていません。その手掛かりを探るため，中山・栗原（2019）は，小学校学習指導要領に対応して作成された新教材（『We Can! 1 』&『We Can! 2 』）において扱われている IC を育む要素を分析しました。その結果，「文化の知識」，「文化への興味」，「文化の多様性に対する知識」などの要素が多く観察されると指摘しました。これらは，小学校学習指導要領の目的にも沿っており，小学校の外国語教育において重点的に扱うことが期待されている要素と解釈できるでしょう。一方，扱われている文化的題材は，表層文化が中心であり，異文化間教育において重要になる「視点の移行」や「文化間の比較」を促す要素の扱いが，限定的

であることも指摘しました。

　教科書という媒体の性質上，目に見える文化が中心に構成されることは自然ですが，単に，国とその知識の産物を結びつけるような指導に終始しては，ステレオタイプを促しかねません。指導者としては，異文化間教育の意義を意識し，教科書にあるたくさんの文化的題材を活用し，児童が自文化とは異なる視点に気づいたり体験したりできる活動へとつなげる工夫が求められます。

IC を育む授業実践

　IC の育成には，自分とは異なる新たな視点の存在に気づき，自文化を相対化する機会を設けることが大切です。ここでいう新たな視点とは，必ずしも外国からの視点とは限りません。文化の定義からも分かるように，異なる視点は国内にも存在します。同じ出来事でも，立場の異なる人から見ると異なって見えることがあり，児童にとって新たな視点になります。

　教科書や教科書付属のデジタル教材に取り上げられている文化を起点に，様々な視点への気づきを促す活動を導入しましょう。その方法としては，比較があります。例えば，教科書では，世界の挨拶のページがあります。これを利用し，日本の挨拶と比較しましょう。相手との距離の取り方や姿勢，接触の有無など様々な違いが発見されます。共通点にも注目しましょう。挨拶の仕方は文化により多様ですが，その目的は他者の尊重など類似点があります。どのような違いがあるのか，推測させたり，調べ学習をさせたりできます。同じ国の中でも相手に応じて異なる挨拶をすることがあること，文化により接触の許容度が異なることなど深層文化への気づきが促されるかもしれません。

　指導を行う際には，児童の発達段階への配慮が必要になります。小学校段階においては，抽象的な思考力は，発達段階にあります。そのため，小学校において文化を扱う際は，知識の学習にとどめず，他者の立場に立つ「体験」ができると理解が深まります。絵本，動画，ロールプレイなどが活用できます。欧州連合の教育を支援する Erasmus ＋ では，早期英語学習に絵本を用いて IC を育もうとするプログラムを展開しています。絵本を利用する理由として，Mourão（2022）は，「教師が注意深く仲介しながら読み聞かせすることで，子

ども達は，普段当たり前と思っていることを他の解釈で理解できるようにな
る。」と説明します。実際の交流も重要です。近年では，国際協働オンライン
学習（Collaborative Online International Learning：COIL）や，紙人形などの実物を
利用した異文化交流活動なども行われています。このフラットスタンレー・プ
ロジェクトでは，自分の紙人形を作り手紙と共に交流先に送ります。交流相手
は，その紙人形を自宅に連れて帰ったり，周囲の名所に連れていったりし，そ
の様子を手紙や写真にまとめます。紙人形は，これらの手紙や写真と共に，日
本に帰国します。このような実物を介した交流は，異文化を児童にとって身近
なものにし，コミュニケーションを行う意欲を高めます。このような「体験」
を通じて身につけた言語は，きっと子どもたちの中に残り，その後の外国語学
習を続ける原動力となることでしょう。

6　Summary & Reflection

A　Summary

Here is a brief summary of the reading part. Fill in the blanks to check your
comprehension.

When you communicate in a foreign language, say English, with someone
from a different cultural background, what ¹(　　　　　　)are needed? It is often
believed that you need linguistic competence, sociolinguistic competence and
pragmatic competences. Then, let's imagine that you became perfect in these
three ²(　　　　　) of communicative competence. Now, do you think you will
not experience ³(　　　　　)?

Recently, the ⁴(　　　　　) of English speakers have become more diverse.
The people you communicate with in English are not always native English
speakers. In other words, even if you master 'native English' norms and language, it does not necessarily mean that your communication partners will understand you as you wish. With this in mind, it is important to develop intercultural competence.

Students in elementary school are still in the ⁵(   ) of learning cultural knowledge. They are flexible and ⁶(   ) about other cultures. Elementary school is a good time to develop students' IC, such as, interest in and ⁷(   ) for other cultures. Teachers should plan English classes with this in mind.

B Reflection

本章では，異文化間でのコミュニケーションを行う際に重要になる概念について学んできました。以下の語句について，具体的な例をあげながら説明してみましょう。

	語　句	説　明
1	Culture 文化	
2	Linguistic Competence 言語能力	
3	Sociolinguistic Competence 社会言語能力	
4	Intercultural Competence 異文化間能力	
5	Intercultural Education 異文化間教育	

Unit 6
Sounds and Spellings

1 Warm-up Activities

A Choose the correct meaning for the following words or phrases using (1) to (10) below.

(　　) sympathize　(　　) exaggeration　(　　) complicated

(　　) phonics　(　　) content　(　　) letter　(　　) exception

(　　) character　(　　) relationship　(　　) admit

---

1 . made of many different things or parts that are connected; difficult to understand：複雑な

2 . a person or thing that is not included in a general statement：例外

3 . a statement or description that makes something seem larger, better, worse, or more important than it really is：誇張表現

4 . a written or printed sign representing a sound used in speech：文字

5 . a letter, sign, mark, or symbol used in writing, in printing, or on computers：アルファベットの文字

6 . to feel sorry for somebody; to show that you understand and feel sorry about somebody's problems：同情する

7 . the subject matter of a book, speech, program, etc：内容

8 . to agree, often unwillingly, that something is true：認める

9 . a method of teaching people to read based on the sounds that letters represent：フォニックス

10. the way in which two people, groups or countries behave towards each other or deal with each other：関係

B Read the following sentences, and check the box in front of each sentence that describes you.

☐ 1 . I am not good at English spelling.

☐ 2 . I often pronounce English words in the wrong way.

☐ 3 . I can imagine the pronunciation of a word from the English spelling.

☐ 4 . I can tell you some of the rules of English sounds and spellings.

☐ 5 . I can identify some exceptions to the rules of English sounds and spellings.

2 Aural & Oral Activities

[A] Read the questions below. Then listen to Track 6-1 and decide whether
each sentence is True（T）or False（F）according to the conversation.

1 . Rie is pleased with her teacher's comments on her English essay. T/F

2 . Steve seems to think English spelling is difficult even for native English
speakers. T/F

3 . Steve was taught phonics when he was a child. T/F

4 . Rie and Steve have different opinions about *kana* characters. T/F

5 . Rie thinks that *kanji* is more difficult than English spelling. T/F

[B] Listen again and fill in the blanks.　　　🎧**Track 6-1** ▶

Rie :　I got my English essay back. I don't know

　　　¹(　　　　　) to be happy or sad about my teacher's comments.

Steve : What do you mean, Rie?

Rie :　He says, "The content is very good, but there are too many spelling mistakes."

Steve : You should be happy about that. And I sympathize with you. English
has a complicated relationship between sounds and spellings. So even
native English speakers like me are ²(　　　　　) phonics from child-
hood.

Rie :　What's that, Steve?

Steve : Phonics. Phonics has a lot of rules, but there are also many

　　　　³(　　　　　　) too.

Rie :　For example, what kind of rules?

Steve : Well,… the spelling of 'phonics' is p-h-o-n-i-c-s. And the two letters 'ph' is pronounced /f/, not /ph/.

Rie :　I know that rule. But it's more like I knew the word and then

　　　　⁴(　　　　　　) the rule later.

Steve : I see. It's ⁵(　　　　　) to understand when you know a lot of words. We've been learning phonics over and over since we were kids. And we have mastered it without knowing it. I was so happy when I could read by myself as a child!

Rie :　I'm so glad my mother tongue is Japanese. In Japanese one *kana* letter has only one sound, so it's hard to make ⁶(　　　　).

Steve : That's true. *Kana* characters are really easy to read. But there are so many *kanji* characters in Japanese. It's hard to live in Japan if you can't read them.

Rie :　That's an exaggeration, Steve. But I admit that *kanji* is as difficult as English spelling.

C Let's try 'Role-Play Shadowing'.

1 . Listen to the Track and check the pronunciation and meaning of each word and sentence.

2 . Try 'Role-Play Shadowing' using the Track with a partner.

3 . Change roles and repeat.

4 . Now role-play with a partner without the Track. Be sure to focus on using the appropriate intonation, rate of utterance, and tone of voice.

D Talk with a partner, and take turns asking and answering the following questions. Then, change partners, and ask and repeat.

1. Do you think English spelling is difficult?

2. What English words do you find difficult to pronounce? Why?

3. Do you know that the alphabet has names and sounds?

4. Have you heard the alphabet jingle?

5. Do you know anything about phonics?

3 Reading Part

A Vocabulary and Phrases

① confuse 混乱させる　②letter 文字　③ *kana* character 仮名文字

④ correspond to ～に一致する　⑤ systematically 体系的に

⑥ explicitly 明示的に　⑦ phoneme 音素　⑧ exception 例外

⑨ sufficient 十分な　⑩ incorporate 取り入れる

B True or False Questions

Read the following statements. After you have read the passage below, answer whether the sentences are True (T) or False (F) according to the passage.

1. Japanese children learn English letters when they start to learn English sounds. T/F

2. Sounds and spellings in English words often differ from word to word. T/F

3. Almost all English words can be pronounced correctly using phonics rules. T/F

4. Phonics instruction is effective when there is sufficient input in English. T/F

5. Phonics is not suitable for Japanese children and does not need to be taught. T/F

C Multiple Choice

After you have read the passage below, choose the right answer to the following questions.

1 . Why is English pronunciation difficult for Japanese children?

  a. The English language has far more sounds than Japanese.

  b. The English language has far fewer sounds than Japanese.

  c. The English language has more sounds than any other language.

2 . How do children in English-speaking countries learn to read words?

  a. They learn to do so naturally by listening to words.

  b. They learn how to read words through picture books.

  c. They are taught how to link sounds and letters using phonics.

3 . What is one of the reasons why phonics instruction may not be effective enough in Japanese classrooms?

  a. There is not enough time to teach phonics.

  b. There are not many teachers who can teach phonics well.

  c. Japanese children are not given enough input in English.

4 . What aspect of phonics can confuse Japanese children?

  a. It has many rules and exceptions.

  b. It is difficult for them to understand its rules.

  c. It is easy for them to understand its rules but difficult to pronounce words.

5 . Which of the following is not mentioned in the passage?

  a. Phonics is an effective way to teach English sounds and spellings.

  b. Phonics should be used in Japan in the same way as in English-speaking countries.

  c. Even if children can read words with phonics, it does not mean that they know what the words mean.

4 Reading Activities

Track 6-2 ▶

Read the following sentences. Listen to the Track, and read it again.

Sounds and Spellings

confuse 混乱させる

become familiar with ～
に慣れ親しむ
letter 文字
kana character 仮名文字
correspond to ～と一致す
る

systematically 体系的に
explicitly 明示的に
phoneme 音素

exception 例外

sufficient 十分な

The first thing that confuses Japanese children when they start learning English is the difficulty in pronouncing English sounds. Since the Japanese language has far fewer sounds than English, it is difficult for Japanese children to hear and pronounce English sounds they have never heard before. After becoming familiar with sounds, they will learn letters. Then, they will come across another difficulty. This is because, while Japanese *kana* characters correspond to one-letter-and-one-sound, there are so many instances in English where the sound and spelling do not match. For this reason, children in English-speaking countries are taught phonics to link sounds and letters from an early age.

Phonics attempts to improve children's ability to pronounce English words correctly by systematically and explicitly teaching the rules for linking phonemes, or the smallest units of sound, to the alphabet. While there are many rules in phonics, there are also many exceptions. The keywords in the exceptions are called 'sight words,' which children must look at and memorize. Since English-speaking children have sufficient input of sounds and letters in their daily lives, phonics instruction allows them to connect sounds and spellings and words they are reading. However, because the amount of English language input in Japanese classrooms is not sufficient, many rules and exceptions can confuse children and cause them to dislike letters. Moreover, even if phonics enables students to pronounce English, it does not help them develop reading skills with an understanding of meaning. Therefore, other instructional methods such as Whole Language Teaching should be used in combination.

At any rate, the children's joy at being able to pronounce English words on their own greatly motivates them to learn English. In conclusion, it is better to make the best use of phonics to the extent that it can be incorporated into Japanese classrooms.

Whole Language Teaching ホール・ランゲージ・ティーチング
at any rate ともあれ
on one's own 自分で

incorporate 取り入れる

5 Mini Lectures

1. 英語の音声とつづり字

音声から文字への指導とは

外国語活動で「聞くこと」と「話すこと」を通して音声に慣れ親しんだ後に，外国語科で「読むこと」，そして「書くこと」へとつなげていきます。ここで，英語に触れるのは教室の中だけというEFL環境で英語を学習する児童が，無理なく音声と文字をつなげていき，読むことができるようになる指導が必要となってきます。

小学校学習指導要領の外国語科，第2　各言語の目標及び内容等には，「（2）読むこと」の目標として次の二つが示されています。

　　ア　活字体で書かれた文字を識別し，その読み方を発音することができるようにする。
　　イ　音声で十分に慣れ親しんだ簡単な語句や基本的な表現の意味が分かるよ

79

うにする。

　アは，アルファベットをその「名称」で発音することができるということで，例えば，a は/ei/，b は/biː/，c は/siː/と発音します。これは，同指導要領の外国語活動，第 2 　各言語の目標及び内容等の「聞くこと」の目標のウ「文字の読み方が発音されるのを聞いた際に，どの文字であるかが分かるようにする。」とつながっています。実際，アルファベットの大文字を 3 年生の後半で，小文字を 4 年生の後半で学習するので，その時点からアルファベットとその名称を結びつける学習が始まっていると言えます。また，イについては，小学校学習指導要領解説には次のように示されています。「英語の文字には，名称と音がある。児童が語句や表現の意味が分かるようになるためには，当然のことながらその語句や表現を発音する必要があり，文字の音の読み方は，そのための手掛かりとなる。したがって，（中略）児童の学習の段階に応じて，語の中で用いられる場合の文字が示す音の読み方を指導することとする。」ここで，アルファベットの音とは，a は/æ/（例：apple）や/ei/（例：station），b は/b/（例：bag），c は/k/（例：cap）や/s/（例：city）のことです。つまり外国語科では，アルファベットには文字の「名称」とは別に「音（おん）」があることを指導する必要があります。そのために，授業の中でアルファベット・ジングルがよく活用されています。アルファベット・ジングルとは，アルファベット順に A から Z の綴りで始まる単語26個を集めて，その語頭の文字を，名称読み→音読み→そのアルファベットで始まる単語の順にリズムに合わせて言います。単語のカテゴリー（例：食べ物，動物，スポーツ）別に多様なバリエーションを作ることもでき，児童が好きな活動の一つになっています。具体的には A，a の文字とりんごのイラストを見ながら，a（/ei/），a（/æ/），a（/æ/），apple（/æpl/）のように名称読みの後に音読みを 2 回繰り返し，その音で始まる単語へとリズミカルに続くので，児童は無意識のうちにアルファベットの音読みに慣れ親しむことができます。

　ここで，音声と文字の関係の指導において留意しておきたいことは，同解説にあるように，「発音と綴りを関連づけて，発音と綴りの規則を指導すること

を意味するものではない」ということです。発音と綴りとを関連付けて指導するのは中学校であり，小学校では音声と文字とを関連付ける指導に留めます。

音声から文字への2つの指導法

　音声と文字を結びつける指導には，大きく分けて二つの方法があります。一つは，ボトムアップ型指導法のフォニックス (Phonics) であり（前述したアルファベット・ジングルはこの指導法に含まれます），**Mini Lectures 2** で詳しく取り上げます。もう一つはホール・ランゲージ・ティーチング (Whole Language Teaching) と呼ばれるトップダウン型の指導法です。前者が音声やスキルを強調するのに対して，後者はその考え方を批判し，体験的に意味を学びながら文字を認知させようとする指導法で，白畑ほか (2019) によると学習者中心の指導法の一つと言えます。この方法では，たくさんの読み聞かせなどを通して音声や文字に出会わせ，その文脈から単語の意味を類推し，読みを学ばせます。現在では，双方のよいところを取り入れた指導法が一般的になっていますが，どちらももともとは子どもが英語を母語として取得する場合の指導法であり，大量の音声と文字によるインプットがあることを前提としているので，日本の小学校の英語の授業で取り入れる場合には，そのような学習環境の違いを十分考慮し，相当の工夫をする必要があります。

2．フォニックスの指導
フォニックスのルールとは

　フォニックスとは，音素（音の最小単位）とアルファベットとの結びつきのルールを体系的・明示的に教えることによって，英単語を適切に発音できる能力を高めようとする指導法です。フォニックスにはたくさんのルールがありますが，紙面の関係で代表的なものを五つ紹介します。

①アルファベット26文字には音がある。

　これは前述のアルファベット・ジングルで説明した通りですが，児童が知っている単語を使ったアルファベット・ジングルの一例を紹介します。

アルファベットの中には二つ以上の音をもつ文字もありますが，ジングルでは1文字1音で示しています。また，xだけは/ks/の音で始まる単語がないため，boxやfoxを使います。

【例】
a, /æ/, apple b, /b/, bear c, /k/, cat d, /d/, dog
e, /e/, egg f, /f/, fish g, /g/, guitar h, /h/, hat
i. /i/, ink j, /dʒ/, jam k, /k/, king l, /l/, lion
m, /m/, milk n, /n/, net o, /ɑ/, orange p, /p/, pig
q, /k/, queen r, /r/, rabbit s, /s/, sun t, /t/, tree
u, /ʌ/, up v, /v/, vest w, /w/, window x, /ks/, box
y, /j/, yacht z, /z/, zebra

a	b	c	d	e	f	g
h	i	j	k	l	m	n
o	p	q	r	s	t	u
v	w	x	y	z		

②単語の終わりが一つの母音＋子音＋eのとき，末尾のeは読まずに，前の母音がアルファベットの名称読みに変わる。

【例】win（勝つ）は①のルールによって/wín/と発音しますが，wine（ワイン）

82

はこのルールにより，i を名称読みして末尾の e を読まないので，/wáin/ と発音します。このルールは，「サイレント e」と呼ばれています。

③二つの子音で新しい音を作る。

【例】ship（船）は sh の 2 文字で /ʃ/ の発音となるので，/ʃíp/ と発音します。

④母音が二つ並ぶと，最初の母音を名称読みし，二つ目は発音しない。

【例】rain（雨）は，ai のうち a を /ei/ と名称読みし，i は発音しないので，/réin/ と発音します。

⑤二つの母音で新しい音を作る。

【例】book（本）は oo の 2 文字で /u/ の発音となるので，/búk/ と発音します。

フォニックスの指導上の留意点

　フォニックスには例外も多く，その場合はサイトワード（sight word）として「目で見て覚える」必要があります。例えば，love, come, some は上述の②「サイレント e」のルールによって o が名称読みの /ou/ と発音されるべきですが，実際には /ʌ/ と発音されます。この他にも，the, my, you, he, and, of などの頻出語があり，これらの重要語はリストにして掲示するなどの工夫が求められます。

　このようにフォニックスにはルールも例外も多いことから，EFL 環境の日本の児童にルールを教えすぎることによって，児童が混乱し，文字を嫌うようになる可能性もあります。また，フォニックスは音読の方法を教えるだけで意味を教えるわけではないので，リーディング力全体をつけることにはならないという指摘もあります。したがって，児童の学習段階に合わせてフォニックスを上手に活用して，「英語が読めた」という喜びを児童が味わえるような指導を行うとともに，意味理解を伴う「読むこと」へとつなげていくことが重要です。

3. 小学校での具体的な指導

フォニックスを活用した指導の土台作り

　フォニックスは，音素とアルファベットとの結びつきのルールを教えることなので，その指導に入る前には，児童が十分な音韻（素）認識能力とアルファベットの知識をもっている必要があります（アレン玉井，2010）。音韻（素）認識能力とは，例えば，cat（猫）の発音が，/k/，/æ/，/t/の三つの音素から成り立っていることが分かる能力のことで，「キャット」としか聞こえない日本の児童にとって最初は分かりにくいかもしれません。このような日本語と英語の音素の違いに気づく手助けになる指導には，ローマ字学習があります。例えば，日本の児童は「か」は一つの音であり，それ以上分けることはできないと思っていますが，ローマ字では「ka」と書かれるのを見て，/k/と/a/という二つの音素がつながって一つの音を作っているということを視覚的に理解することができます。このような理解に至るには児童にある程度のメタ言語力が必要であり，発達段階を考慮して指導することが求められます。したがって，まずは日本語と異なる英語の音声に十分慣れ親しませ，児童の中に英語の音声を十分に蓄積していくことが重要です。そして，児童の反応を見ながら，徐々に文字を与えていきます。例えば，単語の導入の際に，最初はイラストだけのカードを用い，次に綴りを加えます。その際，文字や綴りを指導するのではなく，文字を児童の目に触れさせることによって文字に慣れ親しませ，興味を持たせることを目的とします。このような手順で，まずは英語の音声に，次に文字に十分慣れ親しんだ後に，本格的なアルファベットの指導（形，名称読み，音読み）を行います。これらの土台作りが十分にできているかどうかがフォニックス指導の効果に大きな影響を与えます。

音声と文字の関係の指導の活動例

　上述の土台作りをしながらアルファベット・ジングルに慣れ親しんだ後に取り組める活動例を，易しいものから順に紹介します。

①アルファベットの文字のカード取り

　ペアやグループになり，教師がアルファベット・ジングルに出てきた単語を読み上げ，その語頭音（初頭音）のカードを取らせます。例えば，apple と聞こえたら a のカードを取ります。この活動を通して，アルファベット26文字とそ

の音が正しく結びついているかどうかを確認することができます。

②音を操作する活動

　26の文字とその音が結びついたら，音を操作する活動に移行します。例えば，a と板書して，その音の/æ/を確認した後に，a の後ろに t を板書し，/t/の音を確認します。そして，この2文字の単語 at の音/æt/を確認します。これを数式で表すと a＋t＝at となりますが，音声でも/æ/と/t/をつなげて/æt/と発音できることが重要です。それができたら，at の前に c を板書し，/k/の音を確認します。そして，3文字の単語 cat の発音が，/k/と/æ/と/t/をつなげると「クアット」ではなく/kæt/となることを確認します。この音は日本の児童には「キャット」と聞こえるわけですが，このような指導を通して児童は徐々に音韻（素）認識能力を身につけていくことができます。さらに，語頭の c の文字を b，f，h，m などの文字に替えてできた単語 bat，fat，hat，mat（すべて児童が知っている単語が望ましい）の音を確認していきます。

③絵カードを使って語頭音を区別する活動

　2種類の語頭音の単語で学習済みのものを10個程度選び，絵カード（文字の表記は隠しておく）を準備します。(例：語頭音は/p/と/b/；pan，pen，pig，piano，point，bag，bed，book，bicycle，box)。シャッフルして全員で発音した後に，こ

ゼムクリップ

れらのカードを発音によって二つのグループに分けることを知らせます。教師は4枚程度のカードを順に取り上げ，発音しながら語頭音が/p/のグループは

黒板の右側に, /b/は左側に区別して貼っていきます。そして, 残りのカード を１枚ずつ取り上げ, 全員で発音しながら, どちらのグループに分けるかを尋 ねながら貼っていきます。全部できたら, 共通する語頭音 (/p/と/b/) とその 文字 (pとb) を考えさせます。正解したら, それぞれの絵カードの文字の表 記を見せ, 視覚によっても確認させます。この活動を通して, 日本語では「ペ ン」と「ピッグ」の最初の音は「ペ」と「ピ」で異なりますが, 英語では同じ /p/であるということに児童が気づくことができます。同じような活動を, 異 なる二つの文字 (cとg, tとなど) で行うことができるので, 既習の単語を語 頭音で分類しておくとよいでしょう。

6 Summary & Reflection

A Summary

Here is a brief summary of the readings. Fill in the blanks to check your comprehension.

When Japanese children start to learn to read English, they will have great difficulty. This is because, while Japanese *kana* characters correspond to one-letter-and-one-sound, there are so many instances in English where the sound and spelling do not ¹( ). For this reason, children in English-speaking countries are taught phonics to ²( ) sounds and letters from an early age.

Phonics enables learners to read English words correctly by systematically and explicitly teaching the rules for linking sounds to the alphabet. It has many ³( ) and many ⁴( ) as well. However, since English-speaking children have a sufficient amount of ⁵( ) in terms of English sounds and letters, phonics instruction is very effective for them. In Japanese classrooms, however, many rules and exceptions can confuse children with less input in English. Moreover, it should be noted that phonics does not develop reading skills with an understanding of ⁶( ). Therefore, other instructural methods, for example, Whole Language Teaching should be used in combination with phonics.

　In conclusion, it is desirable to maximize the use of [7](　　　　　) in a way that fits the Japanese classroom environment.

B　Reflection

　本章では，音声とつづり字について学んできました。音声とつづり字の指導に関連する以下の語句について，具体的な例をあげながら説明してみましょう。

	語　句	説　明
1	Phoneme 音素	
2	Alphabet Jingle アルファベット・ ジングル	
3	Phonics フォニックス	
4	Sight Word サイトワード	
5	Whole Language Teaching ホール・ランゲージ・ ティーチング	

Unit 7
Language and Grammar

1 Warm-up Activities

A Choose the correct meaning for the following words or phrases using (1) to (10) below.

( ) envy ( ) unconsciously ( ) upset ( ) order

( ) vocabulary ( ) terrible ( ) proper ( ) genius

( ) praise ( ) memorize

1. unhappy or disappointed because of something unpleasant that has happened：動揺して

2. very unpleasant; making you feel very unhappy, upset or frightened：ひどい

3. to learn something carefully so that you can remember it exactly：暗記する

4. to wish you had the same qualities, possessions, opportunities, etc. as somebody else：うらやましがる

5. all the words that a person knows or uses：語彙

6. right, appropriate or correct; according to the rules：正しい

7. a person who is unusually intelligent or artistic, or who has a very high level of skill, especially in one area：天才

8. the way in which people or things are placed or arranged in relation to each other：順序

9. to say that you approve of and admire somebody / something：ほめる

10. without being aware of something：無意識に

B Read the following sentences, and check the box in front of each sentence that describes you.

☐ 1. Rather than learning grammar, we should first learn a lot of vocabulary.

☐ 2. The best way to learn the grammar of a foreign language is to memorize the grammar rules.

☐ 3. Even if the grammar is wrong, it is good enough to be understood.

☐ 4. It is embarrassing for me to speak using incorrect grammar.

☐ 5. I do not mind if people from other countries speak Japanese using incorrect grammar.

2 Aural & Oral Activities

A Read the questions below. Then listen to Track 7-1 and decide whether each sentence is True (T) or False (F) according to the conversation.

1. Rie is unhappy because she did very badly in her English grammar exam. T/F

2. Rie believes that vocabulary is more important than grammar. T/F

3. Steve speaks both English and French as his first languages. T/F

4. French word order makes learning French grammar easier for English speakers. T/F

5. Steve never studied French grammar for exams through textbooks. T/F

B Listen again and fill in the blanks.　　　🎧**Track 7-1** ▶

Rie : Hi, Steve. I got my French grammar exam back and I'm upset. I got a terrible score. I ¹(　　　) French grammar!

Steve : That's too bad, Rie. I just met Mika and she was happy. She got a good score because she memorized the ²(　　　) textbook.

Rie : I envy her! I think it's better to memorize more words than grammar.

Steve : I think both grammar and vocabulary are important. If the grammar is wrong, you ³(　　　) be able to communicate. Even if you can, you will be seen as someone who cannot use proper language.

Rie : I ^{4}( ). By the way, do you speak French?

Steve : Yes, I do. My mother ^{5}( ) is English, and I learned French as a child. So, I have no problem with it.

Rie : Wow! You are a language genius!

Steve : No, I'm not. French grammar is easy for English speakers. The word order is almost the same.

Rie : Really?

Steve : Yes, and my teachers praised me even when I made grammatical mistakes. I learned French grammar unconsciously from listening to French a lot. Of course, I studied for exams after junior high school.

Rie : How did you study French?

Steve : Well, I read textbooks and tried to understand the grammar rules. Then, I did a lot of grammar ^{6}( ). Maybe the same as you with your English study.

$\boxed{\text{C}}$ Let's try 'Role-Play Shadowing'.

1. Listen to the Track and check the pronunciation and meaning of each word and sentence.

2. Try 'Role-Play Shadowing' using the Track with a partner.

3. Change roles and repeat.

4. Now role-play with a partner without the Track. Be sure to focus on using the appropriate intonation, rate of utterance, and tone of voice.

$\boxed{\text{D}}$ Talk with a partner, and take turns asking and answering the following questions. Then, change partners, and ask and repeat.

1. Are you good at English grammar?

2. How did you learn English grammar?

3. What do you think is the most difficult grammatical matter in English?

4. Do you feel embarrassed when you speak English grammar incorrectly?

5. Do you think even if the grammar is wrong, it is good enough to be understood? Why or why not?

3 Reading Part

A Vocabulary and Phrases

① explicit 明示的な　② child's developmental stage 子どもの発達段階

③ abstract thinking 抽象的思考　④ meta-linguistic ability メタ言語力

⑤ subject 主語　⑥ verb 動詞　⑦ object 目的語　⑧ word order 語順

⑨ grammatical terms 文法用語　⑩ noticing 気づき

⑪ global error グローバルエラー

⑫ implicit corrective feedback 暗示的な修正フィードバック

⑬ recasting 言い直すこと，リキャスト

B True or False Questions

Read the following statements. After you have read the passage below, answer whether the sentences are True (T) or False (F) according to the passage.

1. Whether you can form correct sentences mainly depends on your knowledge of vocabulary. T/F

2. We learn grammar naturally and unconsciously both in first and second language acquisition. T/F

3. It is not always true that grammar should be taught at the early stage of language learning. T/F

4. How to teach grammar to children should be different from teaching it to adults. T/F

5. It is best to correct all of the students' grammatical errors immediately. T/F

C Multiple Choice

After you have read the passage below, choose the right answer to the following questions.

1. Why is grammar important?

   a. It enables us to change the form of words and make sentences.

   b. It can help us learn as many words as possible.

   c. It tells us how to pronounce words.

2. Why is it recommended to start English grammar instruction in the 5th and 6th grades of Japanese elementary school?

   a. Students should learn English grammar before they enter junior high school.

   b. Students need knowledge of grammar to understand the English they learn in these grades.

   c. Students' developmental stages in these grades enables abstract thinking necessary for grammar learning.

3. What is the most important English grammar matter for elementary school students in Japan?

   a. It is to distinguish subject from object.

   b. It is to put subject first, then verb and object in a sentence.

   c. It is to remember grammatical terms such as subject, verb, and object.

4. How should grammar be taught to children?

   a. In a way that grammar rules are first explained with easy grammatical terms.

   b. In a way that sufficient drills help children remember grammatical matters.

   c. In a way that children can notice grammar rules through a lot of input.

5. What should teachers do when they find global errors in their students'

spoken English?

a. They should tell their students immediately that their English is wrong.

b. They should correct their students' errors using implicit feedback.

c. They should ask their students what the meaning is.

4 Reading Activities

🎧 **Track 7-2** ▶

Read the following sentences. Listen to the Track, and read it again.

Grammar and Grammar Instruction

Grammar is the rules in a language for changing the form of words and joining them into sentences; every language has its own grammar. It is an important element of a language because no matter how many words you know, you cannot form sentences without knowing grammar. In the case of a first language, grammar is acquired naturally and unconsciously. In second language acquisition, however, conscious learning of grammar with explicit instruction is effective and essential.

So, when, what, and how should grammar be taught to Japanese children when they learn English as a foreign language? First, the timing of grammar instruction is strongly influenced by the child's developmental stage. It is said that grammar instruction is preferable from the 5th and 6th grades of elementary school, since abstract thinking becomes possible around the age of 11, and then, the meta-linguistic ability to think about the structure of language is ac-

element 要素

no matter how どんなに ～しても

unconsciously 無意識に

explicit 明示的な

child's developmental stage 子どもの発達段階

preferable 望ましい

abstract thinking 抽象的思考

meta-linguistic ability メタ言語力

quired.

word order 語順
subject 主語
verb 動詞
object 目的語

Next, as for what to teach, the highest priority is word order. In other words, students first need to realize that words are placed in the order of subject, verb, and object in English. This is because the word order of Japanese and English is very different, and if the word order is wrong, the meaning will not be understood.

grammatical terms 文法
用語
noticing 気づき
praise ほめる
global error グローバル
エラー
implicit corrective feed-
back 暗示的な修正フィー
ドバック

Lastly, teaching methods should not be the adult approach of explaining rules explicitly with grammatical terms and then giving a lot of grammar exercises. In elementary school, it is best to provide instruction that encourages 'noticing' of grammatical matters while providing sufficient input. And when correcting errors, teachers should first praise the students for using English even if it is grammatically inaccurate, and correct only global errors that do not make sense, using implicit corrective feedback such as recasting.

5 Mini Lectures

1. 文法と文法指導

文法とは？　文法指導とは？

　文法とは，語および語結合における体系のことで，私たちが文法と言われて思い浮かぶものは，学校で国語や英語の授業で習った規範文法（ある個別言語の規則を，その言語の話し手の従うべき規範として述べたもの）であり，学校文法とも呼ばれているものでしょう。一方，「正しい・正しくない」にかかわらず，実生活で使われている様々な文法（例えば，ら抜き言葉など）をそのままをまとめたものを記述文法と言います。また，私たちは母語の文法については，意識せずに使え，明確な説明はできなくても直感で正誤の判断ができますが，この

ような文法知識を暗示的知識（explicit knowledge）と言います。一方，外国語の文法については，文法用語などのメタ言語知識を使って規則を説明した明示的知識（implicit knowledge）を意識的に用いています。したがって，英語の授業における文法指導では英語の規範文法の明示的知識を教えることが主になります。

　では，学習者はどのような段階を経て文法を身につけていくのでしょうか。まず，最初の段階では，学習者は文法規則を理解しますが，Anderson（1983）によると，この段階で獲得する知識を宣言的知識（declarative knowledge）と言います。この知識は，練習することによってその文法事項が使えるようになると次の段階に移行し，この段階で手続き的知識（procedural knowledge）を獲得することになります。さらに練習を重ねることによりその文法事項を素早く正しく使うことができるようになる最終段階では，自動化された手続き的知識を獲得します。したがって，学習者が文法学習につまずいている場合には，これらの３つの段階に応じた適切な指導をする必要があります。例えば，理解ができていない場合には，文法規則を分かりやすく教える必要がありますが，理解はできているが正しく使用できない場合には，宣言的知識を使う練習を繰り返す指導が必要です。文法を習得するためには（第２段階から第３段階に移行する場合は特に）大量の練習をする必要があり，規則を分かりやすく説明する指導力とともに，学習者に飽きさせずに効果的に練習を行わせる指導力が教師に求められます。

　また，文法学習には，規則を身につけた後で様々な事例に対応していく演繹的な学習（deductive learning）と，例の中から規則を導き出す帰納的な学習（inductive learning）があります。一方，特定の項目を意識して学習する明示的学習（explicit learning）と，意識することなく学習する暗示的学習（implicit learning）という分け方もあり，教室で一般的によく行われている教師による文法説明に基づく学習は，演繹的かつ明示的学習となります。そのような文法指導は，効率よく体系的に文法を指導できるという利点がありますが，文法学習のためには暗示的学習を中心にして，明示的学習を補足的に行うことが効果的であると言われています。また，演繹的な指導よりも帰納的な指導の方が学習者の気づき

を促すことができ，言語習得を促進することができるとも言われています。学習者の状況や文法事項によっても事情は異なるため，教室場面に応じてもっとも適切な指導ができるように工夫することが重要です。

小学校英語における文法と文法指導

では，小学校英語での文法または文法指導について考えてみましょう。小学校学習指導要領の外国語科の第1　目標には以下の記述があります。

（2）コミュニケーションを行う目的や場面，状況などに応じて，身近で簡単な事柄について，聞いたり話したりするとともに，音声で十分に慣れ親しんだ外国語の語彙や基本的な表現を推測しながら読んだり，語順を意識しながら書いたりして，自分の考えや気持ちなどを伝え合うことができる基礎的な力を養う。（下線は筆者による）

また，3　指導計画の作成と内容の取扱いの（2）の2の内容の取扱いには，次のような記述があります。

ウ　文や文構造の指導に当たっては，次の事項に留意すること。
　（ア）児童が日本語と英語との語順等の違いや，関連のある文や文構造のまとまりを認識できるようにするために，効果的な指導ができるよう工夫すること。（下線は筆者による）
　（イ）文法の用語や用法の指導に偏ることがないよう配慮して，言語活動と効果的に関連付けて指導すること。

以上のことから，小学校英語における文法では，語順が最重要であること，そして，文法用語や用法を知らなくても，言語活動の中で文法的に正しい英語が使えるようにすることが文法指導として求められていると言えるでしょう。

2.　英語文法の特徴——文構造と名詞

文構造——基本語順は SVO

　日本語と英語の文法の違いの中で，日本人にとってもっとも難しい特徴として文構造の違いが挙げられます。小学校外国語科においても，「文構造」や「語順」という言葉で取り上げられています。英語の基本語順は「SVO：主語＋動詞＋目的語」であり，語順の自由度がほとんどないため，語順によって意味が決まります。例えば，アメリカの教育番組セサミストリートに登場するクッキーモンスターの口癖は「Me love cookies.」です。me は目的格なので通常は文頭に来ることはありませんが，英語の規範文法では文頭の語は主語とみなされるため，I love cookies. の意味で解釈されます。このように実際の英語使用，つまり記述文法では，非標準英語として me を主格として使用することがありますが，くだけた印象を与えるので注意が必要です。

　一方，日本語の基本語順は「SOV：主語＋目的語＋動詞」となりますが，語順の自由度が高く，主語を省略することも頻繁に起こります。前述の「I love cookies.」を日本語の基本語順で言えば「僕はクッキーが大好き。」ですが，「クッキーが大好き。」「大好き，クッキー。」も一般的に通用します。したがって，日本語の語順に慣れている私たちが英語で文を作るときには，「まず主語を置いて，次に動詞，その次に目的語や補語などを置く。」ということを常に強く意識する必要があります。ちなみに，英語を始めヨーロッパの主要言語や中国語は SVO ですが，世界の言語の中で最も多い基本語順は日本語や朝鮮語と同じ SOV なので，英語の語順に苦労しているのは私たち日本人だけではないのです。また，基本語順に加えて，英語では疑問文を作るときにも日本語にはない語順の規則があります。すなわち，基本的には倒置が起こり，主語の前に be 動詞や助動詞を出します。助動詞がない文の場合は，助動詞の do / does / did を主語の前に置き，一般動詞を原形に戻します。そして，疑問詞がある場合は，疑問詞を文頭に置くということも日本語にはない規則です。このように日本語と英語の文構造には大きな違いがありますが，だからこそ，まずは自然な文脈の中で十分な音声のインプットによって慣れ親しむことが重要です。

名詞の用法が複雑

　文構造によって，「私は犬が好きです。」は，I like dogs. であり，I dogs like. / Dogs like I. / Like dogs. は間違いであることが分かりました。では，同じ SVO でも，I like dog. / I like a dog. が正解ではない理由は，名詞の用法にあります。名詞とは物体・物質・人物・場所など具体的な対象を表す語で，英語はそのような対象を大変詳しく説明する言語なので名詞の用法が非常に複雑になっており（大西・マクベイ，2011），日本人にとって難しい文法事項となっています。

　名詞は一般的に，普通名詞（book, pen など），集合名詞（family, police など），物質名詞（water, snow など），抽象名詞（love, peace など），固有名詞（Japan など）の五種類に分けられ，使用において次の三つの観点を考慮する必要があります。①数えられる（可算）か，数えられない（不可算）か，②可算の場合は，単数か複数か，③どういった文脈上の意味（特定・不特定など）があるか，です。①については，普通名詞と集合名詞は可算名詞で，物質名詞，抽象名詞，固有名詞は不可算名詞です。②については，可算名詞の場合は，単数か複数かで区別し，複数の場合は語尾に‐s / es を付けますが，不規則な変化（mouse〈単〉，mice（複））をしたり，単複同形（sheep, deer など）のものもあります。このように単複を区別するのは世界の言語に広く見られる現象で，日本語，朝鮮語，中国語のように区別しない言語の方が少数派です。さらに複雑なのは，集合名詞の場合，集合体を 1 単体として見る用法と，その構成要素である個体を主として見る用法があり，後者の場合は単数でも複数として扱われます。（例：My family *are* all well.）最後に③については，名詞の前に詳細な限定を加える限定詞（a / an, the, many, this など）を置いて，文脈上の意味を明確にします。

　以上から，前述の誤答例である I like dog. / I like a dog. の場合は，① dog は可算名詞なので，② a dog か dogs のどちらかになりますが，1 匹の犬が好きなのではなく，犬というものすべて（総称）が好きなので複数形の dogs が正解となります。ただし，I like dog. を「私は犬の肉が好きです。」という意味を表す不可算名詞で用いることも稀にあり，同じ名詞でも意味によって可算名詞にも不可算名詞にもなることにも注意しなければなりません。（例：paper

は「紙」の意味では不可算名詞ですが，「新聞」の意味では可算名詞です。)

3．小学校での具体的な文法指導

外国語科での文法指導に入る前に

　高学年の外国語科で語順などの文法指導を行う前に，三つの前提条件（①発達段階，②母語における文法学習，③音声による十分なインプットの蓄積）が整っているかどうかを確認するとよいでしょう。まず，①発達段階については，ジャン・ピアジェ（Jean Piaget）の提唱する四つの発達段階のうち，高学年は形式的操作期にあたります。この段階では抽象的に考え，具体物がなくても論理的思考ができるようになり，文法学習に必要とされるメタ言語力（言語に対して客観的に考える力）やメタ認知力（自分の思考や認知に関して客観的に見ることができる力）が身についてきます。中学年はまだ形式的操作期に入っていないため，明示的な文法指導は推奨されません。ただし，子どもの発達段階には個人差があるので，高学年を一律に捉えるのではなく，個々の子どもの発達段階に配慮しながら文法指導を進めていくことが大切です。次に，②母語における文法学習において言葉を抽象的・分析的に処理することができるようになり，文法的な「気づき」の力や知識が母語で育っていれば，英語での文法指導が容易になる可能性が高くなります。したがって，国語における文法学習と関連付けて指導することが効果的です。③音声による十分なインプットの蓄積があれば，抽象的な説明が具体例と結びつきやすく，「ああ，そういうことだったのか。」と容易に理解できます。小学校英語では音声で慣れ親しんだ英語を読んだり書いたりしますが，文法指導でも同様のことが言えます。

「気づき」を促す文法指導

　小学校英語での文法指導でまず押さえておくべきことは，中学校や高等学校でよく行われていた演繹的かつ明示的な指導は適さない場合が多いということです。つまり，最初に規則を提示して明示的に教えることは推奨されません。例えば，6年生での過去形の文法指導を例に挙げて考えてみましょう。演繹的・明示的・体系的な指導では，教師が最初から次のように説明します。「今日は，

動詞の過去形を学習します。『〜した』という過去の意味を表すためには，一般動詞のうち，規則動詞は後ろに－edを付けます。playだったらplayedですね。でも，studyの場合はstudiedとなり，yをiに変えてedを付けます。また，不規則動詞はそれぞれ異なります。例えば，goはwentに，eatはateになります。そして，be動詞のamとisはwasに，areはwereになります。次に，疑問文をつくるときには…。」このようにしてひと通り説明し終わった後，文脈もなく学習者にも関係のない英文を提示して，機械的に過去形に変えていく練習をしたり，英作文をしたりします。このように，学習者は教師から一方的に文法知識を与えられ，一人でドリル練習に励みます。

　では，小学校ではどのようにして過去形を指導したらよいでしょうか。多くの場合，2学期の初めに夏休みにしたことを話し合うという状況を設定した上で，担任とALT（外国語指導助手）がジェスチャーを交えたり写真を提示したりしながら，次のようなやりとりをして導入します。

　担任：Meg-sensei, how was your summer vacation?
　ALT：It was fun!（ジェスチャー）I went to Mt. Aso.（写真の提示）
　担任：Oh, you went to Mt. Aso. What did you do there?
　ALT：I enjoyed camping.（写真の提示）I ate curry and rice.（写真の提示）
　担任：Oh, you enjoyed camping. And, you ate curry and rice. Sounds great!
　ALT：Yes, it was great!（ジェスチャー）

過去形についての説明をしなくても，場面や状況を伴った会話から児童は何となく「wentって聞こえたけど，『行った』ということかな。」「エイトって聞こえたけど，カレーライスと言っていたから，『8』じゃなくて『食べた』ってことかも。」という気づきが生まれてきます。このような「気づき」を促す文法指導が小学校では重要です。そして，十分なインプットを与えて音声で慣れ親しんだ後に，自分のことをペアでやりとりして話す活動へと発展させていきます。そして，児童の発話で文法の誤りがあるときも，明示的に修正するのではなく，リキャスト（recast）によって暗示的修正フィードバックを与え，コ

ミュニケーションを継続しながら「気づき」を促すようにします。例えば，児童が｜阿蘇山に行ったよ。」のつもりで「I go to Mt. Aso.」と言った場合，教師は「Oh, you <u>went</u> to Mt. Aso. I <u>went</u> to Mt. Aso, too.」などと言って会話を継続しながら，児童の「気づき」を促すのです。

6 Summary & Reflection

A Summary

Here is a brief summary of the readings. Fill in the blanks to check your comprehension.

Grammar is the rules in a language for changing the form of words and joining them into [1]( ). In first language acquisition, grammar is acquired naturally and unconsciously. In second language acquisition, however, the conscious learning of grammar with explicit instruction is effective and essential.

So, when, what, and how should grammar be taught to Japanese children when they learn English as a foreign language? First, the child's [2]( ) stage should be considered. Grammar instruction is recommended from the 5th and 6th grades of elementary school, because [3]( ) thinking becomes possible around the age of 11. Thus, the [4]( ) ability needed to think about the structure of language can be acquired. Next, students first need to realize that words are placed in the [5]( ) of subject, verb, and object in English. Finally, teachers should not explain rules explicitly with grammatical terms as they do for adults. In elementary school, teachers should provide instruction that encourages [6]( )' of grammatical matters while providing sufficient [7]( ).

B Reflection

本章では，言語と文法について学んできました。文法と文法指導に関連する以下の語句について，具体的な例をあげながら説明してみましょう。

	語　句	説　明
1	Meta-Linguistic Ability メタ言語力	
2	Word Order 語順	
3	Noticing 気づき	
4	Global Error グローバルエラー	
5	Implicit Corrective Feed-Back 暗示的な修正フィードバック Recast リキャスト	

Unit 8
Children's Literature ①

1 Warm-up Activities

[A] Choose the correct meaning for the following words or phrases using (1) to (10) below.

(   ) character   (   ) nursery rhyme   (   ) fun   (   ) the original

(   ) version   (   ) translation   (   ) picture book

(   ) let me see   (   ) prefer something to another thing

(   ) recommend

---

1 . a piece of work containing many illustrations, especially for children：
絵本

2 . enjoyable, amusing：楽しい，おもしろい

3 . a piece of work that has been changed from one language into another：
翻訳

4 . short verses and songs for children：わらべ歌，韻文で書かれた子ども
向けの話

5 . not a copy; created by a particular writer：原作

6 . used when you are considering your next words：(会話などで) そうねえ

7 . a person or an animal in a story, novel, play, or movie：登場人 (動) 物

8 . a particular edition of a book or a work：(文学作品などの) 版

9 . advise someone to do something：人に何かをすることを勧める

10. like something better than another thing：何かを別のことよりも好む

[B] Read the following sentences, and check the box in front of each sentence that describes you.

☐ 1 . When I was a child, I read many picture books.

□ 2. I prefer reading books online to reading them on paper.

□ 3. I have experienced reading a book / books in English.

□ 4. I know the story of a young girl named Alice who went down a rabbit-hole.

□ 5. Reading stories in English is difficult.

□ 6. I know an English song written for children.

2 Aural & Oral Activities

[A] Read the questions below. Then listen to Track 8-1 and decide whether each sentence is True (T) or False (F) according to the conversation.

1. Rie once read Alice's picture book in English. T/F

2. Lewis Carrol is a British writer. T/F

3. Rie is not interested in the original story of Alice. T/F

4. Steve thinks that Rie should read *Alice's Adventures in Wonderland* in Japanese. T/F

5. Humpty Dumpty is a character originally created by Lewis Carrol. T/F

[B] Listen again and fill in the blanks.　　　🎧Track 8-1 ▶

Rie :　What are you reading, Steve?

Steve : I am reading *Alice's Adventures in Wonderland*. Do you know this story?

Rie :　Of course! I read Alice's ¹(　　　　　)book when I was little. But it was written in Japanese.

Steve : Maybe, you read the Japanese translation of Alice's story. The original ²(　　　　　) was written by the British writer Lewis Carroll.

Rie :　Oh, I did not know that. I hope to read the original. Would it be difficult for me?

Steve : Well, I don't think so.

Rie :　Let me ³(　　　　　). Ah, there are many difficult words. But I can understand what happens in the story.

Steve : Great! I recommend that you read the original. You can meet many interesting ⁴(   ).

Rie : I know this cat; it's the Cheshire-Cat. Hmm…I know this egg; it's Humpty Dumpty.

Steve : Actually, Humpty Dumpty is not a character created by Lewis Carroll.

Rie : What do you mean?

Steve : Humpty Dumpty comes ⁵(   ) a nursery rhyme that goes like this :

Humpty Dumpty sat on a wall,

Humpty Dumpty had a great ⁶(   ).

All the king's horses,

And all the king's men,

Couldn't put Humpty together again.*

Rie : What a fun song!

* (Opie & Opie, 1997)

C Let's try 'Role-Play Shadowing'.

1. Listen to the Track and check the pronunciation and meaning of each word and sentence.

2. Try 'Role-Play Shadowing' using the Track with a partner.

3. Change roles and repeat.

4. Now role-play with a partner without the Track. Be sure to focus on using the appropriate intonation, rate of utterance, and tone of voice.

D Talk with a partner, and take turns asking and answering the following questions. Then, change partners, and ask and repeat.

1. Which do you like better, reading books online or on paper? Why?

2. Which do you like better, reading books or watching movies? Why?

3. What are the advantages and disadvantages of reading stories that are

translated in other languages?

4. What can we learn from the literature of other countries ?

5. What nursery rhymes did you sing when you were a child?

3 Reading Part

A Vocabulary and Phrases

① objective 目標　② foundation 基礎　③ literary work 文学作品
④ table 表　⑤ grade 学年　⑥ context 文脈　⑦ function 機能　⑧ lexis 語彙
⑨ syntax シンタックス，句・節・文の構成（法）　⑩ phonology 音韻（論）

B True or False Questions

Read the following statements. After you have read the passage below, answer whether the sentences are True (T) or False (F) according to the passage.

1. Elementary school English education has reduced the use of children's literature for a long time. T/F

2. Children's literature provides a meaningful context to learn English. T/F

3. Jonathan Swift wrote *The Happy Prince*. T/F

4. Students can express their ideas and enjoy talking with their friends after reading literary works. T/F

5. There is no possibility of using literary materials in English education in universities. T/F

C Multiple Choice

After you have read the passage below, circle the correct statements in each group.

1. a. The goals of English education in elementary schools have little to do with the goals of English education in universities.

   b. The goals of English education in elementary schools have nothing to do with the goals of English education in universities.

c. The goals of English education in elementary schools have much to do with the goals of English education in universities.

2 . a. When teachers ask questions about stories, they should always expect the same answer from students.

b. When teachers ask questions about stories, they should sometimes expect different answers from students.

c. When students answer questions about stories, they sometimes repeat the same patterns.

3 . a. English translations of old Japanese stories are used in elementary school English textbooks.

b. English translations of old stories from India are used in elementary school English textbooks.

c. English translations of old Egyptian stories are used in elementary school English textbooks.

4 . a. *The Very Big Turnip* is used as a Foreign Languages textbook only for Grade 5 students.

b. *The Very Big Turnip* is used as a Foreign Languages textbook only for Grade 6 students.

c. *The Very Big Turnip* is used as a Foreign Languages textbook for both Grades 5 and 6 students.

5 . a. Nowadays, university English education actively uses literary materials to improve students' communication abilities.

b. Nowadays, elementary school English education actively uses literary materials to improve students' communication abilities.

c. Nowadays, both university and elementary school English education actively use literary materials to improve students' communication abilities.

4 Reading Activities

 Track 8-2 ▶

Read the following sentences. Listen to the Track, and read it again.

Children's Literature and Elementary School English Education

overall 全般的な
nurture 育成する
literary materials 文学教材
A Bundle of Sticks イソップ（Aesop）物語『小枝の束』
The Story of the Zodiac 中国昔話『十二支の話』
The North Wind and the Sun イソップ物語『北風と太陽』
Twelve Months スロバキア昔話『12か月』
A Good Idea! 奈街三郎『はしの上のおおかみ』
The Gingerbread Man アメリカ昔話『ジンジャー・ブレッドマン』
Who's Behind Me? ふくだあきこ・ふくだとしお『うしろにいるのだあれ』

The overall objective of elementary school English education is to nurture the foundation of children's communication skills. Children's literature has been used for English classes in elementary schools for a long time.

With this background in mind, what kinds of literary works are used in English classrooms? Tables 1 and 2 show examples of literary materials in Foreign Languages textbooks for Grades 5 and 6 students.

Table 1   *Stories for Grade 5 students*

Text*	Title
NH	*A Bundle of Sticks*
JS	*The Story of the Zodiac*
JT	*Shaggy's Story*
CJ	*The North Wind and the Sun* *Twelve Months* *The Happy Prince*
OW	*A Good Idea!*
HW	*The Gingerbread Man*
BS	*Who's Behind Me?*

Table 2　*Stories for Grade 6 students*

Text*	Title
NH	*Butterfly Friends*
JS	*The Story of Vega* *The Very Big Turnip*
JT	*Shaggy's Story*
CJ	*The Gulliver's Travels* *The Blue Bird* *Mary Had a Little Lamb*
OW	*A Great Idea!* *The Letter*
HW	*The Rolling Rice Ball* *Kurikindi*
BS	*The Very Big Turnip*

*NH = *New Horizon Elementary English Course*, JS = *Junior Sunshine*, JT = *Junior Total English*, CJ = *Crown Jr.*, OW = *One World Smiles*, HW = *Here We Go!*, BS = *Blue Sky Elementary*

As you can see, some of the stories in the tables are well-known examples of children's literature. For instance, *The Happy Prince* was written by Oscar Wilde, while *The Gulliver's Travels* was written by Jonathan Swift. Originally, *Mary Had a Little Lamb* is not a story but a famous nursery rhyme.

Then, how can children's literature contribute to elementary school English teaching? First, it embeds a meaningful context of learning English. Such a context can help learners gain a deeper understanding of linguistic forms and linguistic functions. Second, most examples of children's literature employ repeated patterns in terms of lexis, syntax, phonology, and discourse. Third, stories enable teachers to ask their stu-

Butterfly Friends ドイツ昔話『チョウの友達』

The Story of Vega 中国昔話『七夕の話』

The Very Big Turnip ロシア昔話『大きなかぶ』

The Blue Bird ベルギー作家メーテルリンク（Maeterlinck）『青い鳥』

A Great Idea! 小野瀬稔『およげないりすさん』

The Letter アーノルド・ローベル（Arnold Lobel）『お手紙』

The Rolling Rice Ball 日本昔話『おむすびころりん』

Kurikindi エクアドル昔話『クリキンディ』

embed　〜を埋め込む

employ　用いる
discourse　談話（文よりも長く，まとまりを持った単位）

dents certain questions that may not have only one right answer, and encourage learners to create meaningful answers from the text. Furthermore, students can use literary works to express their thoughts freely and have lively discussions with friends.

Recently, university English classrooms have reduced the use of literary materials considering the current overall objective of English teaching in Japan which is to develop students' communication skills in English. However, if we analyze why and how literary materials are used in elementary school, we can find many possibilities for using these materials, along with the benefits for university students.

5 Mini Lectures

1. 英語圏の児童文学

児童文学は誰のものなのか

児童文学とは，いったい誰のために書かれた作品を指すのでしょうか。学校教育法をはじめとする条文や文部科学省が発信する文書を見ると，園児（幼稚園生），児童（小学生），生徒（中学・高校生），学生（大学や専門学校生）という区別が一般的にされています。「児童」の時代を過ぎた皆さんは，児童文学を読む資格はないのでしょうか。

児童文学の研究者として名高いピーター・ハント（Peter Hunt）は，児童文学（children's literature）を「texts for children」と三語で定義した上で，これら三語の意味は柔軟に扱わなければならないと説明しています（Hunt, 2001）。「子どもの・ための・テキスト」とは言うものの，その意味づけは作品を送り出す作者や，作品を受けとめる読者によって，様々に変わるのです。

英語圏はどこを指すのか

　英語圏という表現も曖昧です。仮に英語圏を「大多数の人々が英語を母語にする国」ととらえると，英国・米国・カナダ・オーストラリア・ニュージーランドなどが思い浮かぶかもしれません。英語を公用語としている国まで入れると，インド・フィリピン・シンガポール・ケニア・ガーナなど，さらに多くの国に範囲が広がります。児童文学を小学校英語教育で扱う時，いったいどの地域の文学作品を含めればよいのでしょうか。

　小学校で英語を教える意義は，世界の英語（world Englishes）の担い手を育てるということです。小学校英語検定教科書や，小学校で活用されている英語教材を見ると，いろいろな国の子どもたちが登場することに気づくと思います。児童文学を扱う際には，英国や米国生まれの作品に偏り過ぎることなく，原文を英訳した作品も含めて幅広い児童文学に目を向けたいものです。このような視点に立つ時，日本に昔から伝わる話の英訳版を使うこともよい考えです。実際，小学校英語授業では，「桃太郎」や「おむすびころりん」などの日本昔話の英訳版が，教材として活用されてきました。日本特有の文化が，英語ではどのように表現可能かを考えることを通して，日本語・日本文化の特色や豊かさに気づくきっかけにもなるでしょう。

大人になった皆さんと，児童文学

　たまには近くの図書館や書店に行って，児童書コーナーを覗いてみませんか。皆さんが幼いころに読んだ絵本や，懐かしい児童書が見つかるかもしれません。優れた文学作品は，時代を経て，いつまでも読まれ続けます。昔出会った作品を大人になってもう一度手に取る時，心豊かになる瞬間がきっとあるはずです。以前大好きだった作品を，五年後十年後に再び読んでみたら，最初は気づかなかった一文に，強く心がひかれることがあるでしょう。逆に，昔はとても感動したお話を改めて読み返すと，そこまで魅力を感じないこともあるでしょう。過去の自分を振り返り，現在の自分を見つめなおす──心に残る文学作品は，私たちにとって，言わば定点観測の役割を果たしてくれます。

　児童文学は，子どもたち専用の作品ではなく，小学校英語教育を担う皆さん

にとっても大切な意味を持ちます。英語で書かれたお気に入りの文学作品を見つけて，将来，子どもたちに読み聞かせてあげたら，きっと豊かな時間が教室に流れることでしょう。

2. 小学校英語教育と児童文学

検定教科書の中の児童文学

　2019年度から大学教職課程で始まった，小学校「外国語（英語）コア・カリキュラム」は，「小学校における外国語活動・外国語の授業を担当するために必要な背景的な知識」の一つに，「児童文学（絵本，子ども向けの歌や詩等）」を含めています（東京学芸大学，2017）。

　それでは，小学校英語教育では，どのような児童文学が用いられているのでしょうか。2020年度から使用されている「外国語」（英語）の検定教科書（5・6年生対象）では，会話教材（例えば，自己紹介・道案内・飲食店での注文など）が多く採用されています。一方，会話教材の数には及ばないものの，すべての教科書に児童文学が掲載されています。以下では，小学校英語教育を担う皆さんが，どのような児童文学にふれておけばよいのかについて，検定教科書の内容を踏まえて考えていきます。

検定教科書で使用されている物語

　先述したように，2020年度から使用されている検定教科書すべてが，児童文学作品を採用しています。実際に教科書を見ると，絵本・物語の採用数が多いことが分かります。絵本は「文字と挿絵が一体化した物語」と見なすことが可能ですので，以下では絵本と物語を同じ意味で使うことをあらかじめお断りしておきます。

　物語教材1件につき与えられた頁数は，教科書によって幅があり，単元（Lessonや Unit）の中で扱うか否か，発展的な内容と見なすか否かも，各教科書で判断が分かれています。物語教材と共に掲載されている問いや活動に関しては，教材ごとに細やかな問い・活動を用意している例がある一方で，全物語に同じ問い・活動が付された例もあります。

　物語の出典は多岐にわたり，日本昔話（『おむすびころりん』）や起源は中国ですが日本文化に根ざした話（十二支や七夕の物語），日本語で書かれた絵本の英訳版（『Who's Behind Me?』），世界各地の昔話・物語（『A Bundle of Sticks』，『The North Wind and the Sun』，『The Happy Prince』，『The Gingerbread Man』，『The Very Big Turnip』，『The Gulliver's Travels』，『The Blue Bird』），他教科教材として子どもになじみ深い物語（『The Letter』），新たに創作された物語（『Shaggy's Story』）もあります。どの教材にも共通する特色は，挿絵が多い点で，中には 4 ～ 8 コマを用いて漫画仕立てにしている教材もあります（髙橋，2022）。

　これまで見たように，小学校で用いられている物語は，英語圏由来のものに留まりません。日本昔話や英語圏以外の物語も多く含まれます。これから小学校英語教育を担う皆さんは，幅広い地域で語り継がれてきた子ども向けの物語への興味や関心を高め，異文化理解に努めておくと安心です。

検定教科書で使用されている歌・詩

　検定教科書で扱われている児童文学は，物語だけではありません。歌と題した教材をすべての単元に掲載する教科書があったり，少数の歌を扱う教科書があったりします。歌を扱う場合，大多数は歌詞を教科書に掲載していますが，歌のタイトルのみ記載する例もあります。また，歌は英語を楽しんで学ぶ教材と捉え，物語や詩と共に発展扱いで掲載している教科書もあります。

　選ばれている歌は，昔から親しまれてきたナーサリー・ライムが多く見られます（『Pat-A-Cake』や『London Bridge』，『Pease Porridge Hot』，『Humpty Dumpty』など）。一方，『We Are the World』のように比較的新しい歌を取り入れる場合もあります。

　ここでナーサリー・ライムの意味を，改めて確認しておきましょう。広い意味では，伝承童謡を指し，18世紀末にイギリスやアメリカで出版されたマザー・グース（Mother Goose）は中でも有名な例としてあげられます。先述したコア・カリキュラム策定時に，マザー・グースを特に取り上げて扱うことに対して賛否両論がありました。結果的には，コア・カリキュラム最終案では「児童文学（絵本，子ども向けの歌や詩等）」という表現に落ち着いた経緯があります（東京

学芸大学，2017）。このような背景はあるものの，複数の教科書で活用されている実態を踏まえると，マザー・グースが英語圏で果たしてきた役割を知っておくことはとても大切です。よく知られる歌とともに伝え継がれてきた手遊びなどの動作も学習することを通して，異文化理解への学びを深めることが可能です。

　児童文学には，各作品の歴史的背景や，長い時間をかけて育まれてきた文化が込められています。これらの背景・文化の存在を知り，価値を認めることが出来た時，はじめて児童文学を用いた英語教育を担えるのです。検定教科書における児童文学を核としながらも，この外に広がる豊かな歴史・文化について，興味や関心を持つことが大切です。まずは今回言及した児童文学作品を実際に手に取って，楽しみながら読んでみましょう。

3．文学作品の特色
物語の特色

　最後に物語に焦点を当てて，その特色を考えていきます。物語には多くの特色があります。会話教材にはなかなか出てこない豊かな言葉が使われていたり，様々な国の文化を感じ取れたりする点も大きな特色です。ここでは，豊かな文脈，繰り返される表現／場面，そして多彩な解釈に絞って述べていきます。

豊かな文脈

　物語には背景（setting）があり，登場人物や動物（characters）が問題に直面し，問題解決を目指してプロット（plot）を構築していきます。このような構造を持つ物語は，一つひとつの出来事を積み重ねながら文脈を形成していきます。例えば，英訳版「桃太郎」を用いる場合，この話は日本語を母語とする児童の大多数が知っているため，子どもたちのスキーマ（schema）を活用して一定の文脈の中で英語を教えることが期待できます。桃太郎が鬼の悪事を目の当たりにした場面では「He is angry.」，鬼に勝利した場面では「He is happy.」と，それぞれの文脈を踏まえて感情を表す表現を教えることが可能です。このような利点は，もちろん外国の物語からも得ることができます。例えば『The

Snow White（白雪姫）』には，「世界で一番美しい人は白雪姫だ」と鏡から聞かされて，継母が激怒する場面がありますね。もしも子どもたちがこの物語を知っているならば「She is angry.」という表現を文脈の中で教えることができるのです。白雪姫が生き返った場面では「They are happy.」という表現を結びつけることも可能でしょう。物語は豊かな文脈に支えられているため，どの場面を選び出しても登場人物がどのような感情を抱くのかが想像しやすく，教えたい表現を機械的に教えることから逃れることができるのです。

繰り返される表現／場面

　文部科学省が作成した 3 年生の教材『Let's Try! 1』に掲載されている「Who are you?」（Unit 9）には，どのような繰り返しが見られるでしょうか。まず，「I see something....」という表現が何度も現れます。something の後には色や大きさを表す形容詞が続きます。これら形容詞は white ⇔ black などの反意語が順次出て来ます。ほかの表現上の繰り返しには，犬の問いかけ（「Are you a rabbit?」など）と，相手の動物の返答があります。見つかってしまった動物の返事を通して，種々の動物に応じた体の部位（ears, eyes, head など）が出て来るパターンが繰り返されます。これまで見たように，繰り返し同じ表現が用いられる物語は，言わばパタン・プラクティス（pattern practice）を内包しています。従来，パタン・プラクティスは，基本的な英語の型を学習する利点がある一方，機械的な文型練習になると批判を浴びることもありました。一方，物語には豊かな文脈が伴うため，例え同じ表現が繰り返し現れたとしても，豊かなパタン・プラクティスの実践が可能になるのです。

　次に内容面の繰り返しを見てみましょう。この物語は森の中で動物たちがかくれんぼをして遊んでいる場面を扱っています。オニ役の犬が，隠れている動物たちの体の一部を見て，どの動物かを推測しながら次々と相手を見つけていきます。この「探しては見つける」という繰り返しを通して，子どもたちは次に来る内容を推測することが可能です。そして最後はこの型を崩して，竜が動物たちの頭上から現れるという意外な展開が用意されています（文部科学省，2018）。

「Who are you?」に見られるように，表現面でも内容面でも一定の型が繰り返される物語を用いる場合，英語に親しみやすく，内容が推測・理解しやすい授業展開が期待できます。

多彩な解釈

物語を教材として用いる場合，客観的な解釈を行うだけではなく，主観的な解釈を行う可能性が高まります。客観的な解釈とは，物語のある箇所を根拠として意味を解釈できる場合を指し，そこには同一の解釈しかありません。一方，主観的な解釈では，一人ひとりが物語から感じ取る意味や想像する領域を大切にするため，十人十色の解釈がありえるのです。例えば，登場人物を指さして「Who is he / she?」と問いかける場合の答は一つです。一方，「Is he / she happy?」と聞いた場合，子どもたちの主観が反映される可能性が高く，答は一つとは限りません。異なる意見が出た場合，その根拠を尋ねる機会が生まれてさらに対話が発展していきます。皆が同じ意見を持った場では，活発な対話は生まれにくいものですが，異なる意見が生まれる際は，双方向的な (interactive) やり取りが生まれる可能性が高まります。教師⇔子どもたち，子どもたち⇔子どもたちのやり取りが活発に行われることが期待できます。

本節では，物語の特色を中心に考えました。これらの特色は，子ども向けの歌や詩を用いた場合にも当てはまる可能性が高いと言えます。皆さんのお気に入りの文学作品を対象にして，どのような特色が見られるのか，ぜひ分析してみましょう。きっと新しい発見があるはずです。

6 Summary & Reflection

A Summary

Here is a brief summary of the readings. Fill in the blanks to check your comprehension.

The overall objective of elementary school English education is to develop a foundation of children's [1]( ) skills. Related to this, children's literature has been used in English classes at elementary school for a long time. Such works, that are used in elementary schools, are not limited to those from ²(　　　　)-speaking countries. In fact, literature from all over the world has been used for educating children who are expected to use ³(　　　　) Englishes in the future.

How does children's literature contribute to teaching English in elementary school? First, a meaningful ⁴(　　　　) of learning English is embedded within the literary materials. Such a (　4　) can give learners a deeper understanding of linguistic forms and linguistic functions. Second, repeated ⁵(　　　　) in terms of lexis, syntax, phonology, and discourse exist across most literary works. Third, when elementary school teachers use literary works for teaching English, they can set questions that may not have only one ⁶(　　　　) answer, and encourage children to derive meanings from texts. Furthermore, students can use literary works to express their thoughts freely and interact with their friends.

B Reflection

本章では，児童文学を，英語圏の文学，検定教科書で扱われている文学，文学作品の特色の観点から学んできました。児童文学に関連する以下の語句について，具体的な例をあげながら説明してみましょう。

	語　句	説　明
1	Context （豊かな）文脈	
2	Repeated Pattern（s） （豊かな）パターンプラクティス	

3	Subjective Interpretation 主観的な解釈 Objective Interpretation 客観的な解釈	
4	Nursery Rhymes わらべ歌 Mother Goose マザー・グース Humpty Dumpty ハンプティダンプティ	
5	Children's Literature of the English-Speaking World 英語圏の児童文学 Children's Literature of the World 世界の児童文学	

Unit 9
Children's Literature ②

1 Warm-up Activities

A Choose the correct meaning for the following words or phrases using (1) to (10) below.

(   ) castle   (   ) indispensable   (   ) practice   (   ) speaking of
(   ) grade   (   ) fairy tale   (   ) square   (   ) worry about
(   ) such as   (   ) ignorant of

---

1. to be anxious about someone：～を心配する

2. for example：例えば～

3. to say more about a subject that someone has just mentioned：～と言えば

4. absolutely necessary：絶対に必要な，なくてはならない

5. not knowing facts that you ought to know：～を知らない

6. those pupils in a school who are grouped by age：学年

7. a large, strong building with thick high walls and towers built by the people of kings or queens：城

8. an open area surrounded by buildings in a town：広場

9. to do an activity to improve a skill：練習する

10. a children's story in which magical things happen：おとぎ話

B Read the following sentences, and check the box in front of each sentence that describes you.

☐ 1. I have experienced learning English together with children.

☐ 2. I have experienced learning English through literary works.

☐ 3. I once read a fairy tale about a prince or a princess.

□ 4. I know the story of *The Happy Prince*.

□ 5. Money is indispensable to be happy.

2 Aural & Oral Activities

[A] Read the questions below. Then listen to Track 9-1 and decide whether each sentence is True (T) or False (F) according to the conversation.

1. Rie joined an English class for the 4th grade students. T/F

2. When Rie joined an English class, the children were learning how to count numbers. T/F

3. Rie thought that the children were very happy in the English class. T/F

4. Rie was not familiar with the story of *The Happy Prince*. T/F

5. The Happy Prince still lives in the castle, completely ignorant of people's lives. T/F

[B] Listen again and fill in the blanks.   🎧**Track 9-1** ▶

Rie :   I went to an elementary school yesterday.

Steve : Good. Did you study with children?

Rie :   Yes. I joined an English class for the 3rd ¹(   ) students.

Steve : What were they learning?

Rie :   They practiced saying, "Hello. How are you?" Then, they answered using phrases such ²(   ) "I'm fine." And "I'm happy." They looked very happy.

Steve : That's good to hear. ³(   ) of being 'happy', do you know the story of *The Happy Prince*?

Rie :   No, I don't. Is it a famous story?

Steve : It is. I think you can find this story in one of the elementary school English textbooks.

Rie :   I guess it is about a prince who has everything and lives in a beautiful ⁴(   ).

Steve : Not really, he stands in a town square and worries ⁵(　　　　　) poor

people.

Rie :　He stands outside? Why? There is no ⁶(　　　　　) he can be happy.

C Let's try 'Role-Play Shadowing'.

1 . Listen to the Track and check the pronunciation and meaning of each word
and sentence.

2 . Try 'Role-Play Shadowing' using the Track with a partner.

3 . Change roles and repeat.

4 . Now role-play with a partner without the Track. Be sure to focus on using
the appropriate intonation, rate of utterance, and tone of voice.

D Talk with a partner, and take turns asking and answering the following
questions. Then, change partners, and ask and repeat.

1 . What materials do you often use when learning English?

2 . What are the advantages and disadvantages of learning English through literary works?

3 . What is the difference between stories and everyday conversations?

4 . What is the most impressive story you have ever read?

5 . What do you think are the conditions for happiness?

3 Reading Part

A Vocabulary and Phrases

① pros and cons　賛否両論　② circulate　噂などが広がる

③ feature　特色　④ criteria（criterion の複数形）基準

⑤ medium　伝達の手段となる媒体（複数形は media）　⑥ polysemy　多義性

⑦ discourse　談話（文よりも長く，まとまりを持った言語単位）

⑧ diagram　図表　⑨ multiple　多様な　⑩ conventionally　伝統的に，慣例的に

B True or False Questions

Read the following statements. After you have read the passage below, answer whether the sentences are True (T) or False (F) according to the passage.

1. Every person believes that the English language used in literature is unique. T/F

2. From Carter and Nash's viewpoint, literary language is not unique. T/F

3. 'Literariness' measures whether a text has literary characteristics. T/F

4. In a text with many polysemic features, most words have only one meaning. T/F

5. Texts conventionally regarded as non-literary do not have literary characteristics at all. T/F

C Multiple Choice

After you have read the passage below, circle the correct statements in each group.

1. a. Literary English has always been regarded as unique.

   b. Literary English has never been regarded as unique.

   c. Literary English is sometimes regarded as unique.

2. a. If a text does not use any media except the written word, it can be considered medium dependent.

   b. If a text does not use any media except the written word, it can be considered medium independent.

   c. If a text uses various media except the written word, it can be considered medium independent.

3. a. Re-registration measures whether a text incorporates a different type of text.

   b. Re-registration measures whether a text uses different types of media.

c. Re-registration measures whether a text has words with many meanings

4. a. Polysemy is one of the criteria proposed by Carter and Nash.

b. Polysemy is a way of counting the number of words.

c. Polysemy is a criterion for judging first impressions.

5. a. Texts conventionally regarded as non-literary can have literary characteristics.

b. Texts conventionally regarded as literary cannot have literary characteristics.

c. Texts conventionally regarded as non-literary cannot have literary characteristics.

4 Reading Activities　🎧Track 9-2 ▶

Read the following sentences. Listen to the Track, and read it again.

Is Literary English Really 'Special'?

Do you think the English language used in literature is special? Regarding the uniqueness of literary language, pros and cons have been circulating for a long time. On the one hand, it is generally asserted that literary language is unique compared with other kinds of texts. On the other hand, it is firmly believed that literary language is common and cannot be separated from language in different text types such as conversations and expository texts.

Carter and Nash's opinions (1990) have influenced literary stylistics. They believe that literary language is

regarding ～について言えば

assert ～と断言する

expository texts 説明文

Carter and Nash 英語の文体を教育に生かすために研究をした学者

stylistics 文体論

formal（言語の）形式の
上での
medium dependence（文
字以外の）媒体に依存す
ること
re-registration（ほかのタ
イプのテクストを）新た
に集録すること
semantic density 意味の
密度
displaced interaction 変
異相互作用（作者と読者
の関係が変化すること）
bar 妨げる
admission 受け入れられ
ること
incorporate 組み入れる
lexical item 語彙項目
interpretant（語彙などに
対する）解釈，意味の取
り方
layers of meaning 意味の
層

not unique and should be measured by the formal feature of 'literariness'.

In their work, Carter and Nash set up six criteria for judging literariness: medium dependence, re-registration, semantic density, displaced interaction, polysemy, and discourse patterning. Let us focus on three criteria. First, medium dependence indicates that 'the more literary a text' will be, 'the less it will be dependent for its reading on another medium or media.' Examples include illustrations, photographs, pictures, and diagrams. Second, re-registration shows that 'no single word or stylistic feature or register will be barred from admission to a literary context.' Literature can incorporate many words and stylistic features from different text types. Finally, one characteristic of the polysemic text is that 'its lexical items do not stop automatically at their first interpretant.' In other words, the language used in literary texts often has multiple layers of meaning (Carter & Nash, 1990).

Therefore, according to Carter and Nash, texts conventionally regarded as non-literary can have literary qualities.

5 Mini Lectures

1. 文学の言葉

文学の言語は特別なのか

　文学作品で用いられている言語は特別・特殊であるか否か，日常的に使用されている言語と区別するべきか否か。この議論は古くて新しいと言えるでしょ

う。中でも注目したいのは，教育的文体論（pedagogical stylistics）で，この文体論に則った理論の一つがロナルド・カーター（Ronald Carter）とウォルター・ナッシュ（Walter Nash）が説いた「文学らしさ（literariness）」の概念です。カーターたちは，「文学らしさ」はどのようなテクストにも存在していて，個々のテクストの文学性は程度の差だと説明しました。

文学らしさとは——三つの基準を中心に

　カーターたちは，「文学らしさ」を測るために六つの基準（medium dependence, re-registration, semantic density, displaced interaction, polysemy, discourse patterning）を示しました（Carter & Nash, 1990）。例えば，「媒体依存度（medium dependence）」とは，挿絵や写真，図表などをテクストでどの程度用いているかに注目し，これらに頼っているテクストは文学性があまり見られないテクスト，逆にこれらに頼らないテクストは文学性が含まれるテクストだと説明しています。大学入試問題を例にして，この点を考えてみましょう。かつての大学入試問題は文字中心で，現在よりも物語教材が多く出題されました。一方，最近の入試問題は，会話や説明文・論説文などが主体になり，様々な図表やイラストがふんだんに用いられています。したがって，「媒体依存度」の観点から見ると，入試問題から文学らしさが失われたと言えるでしょう。

　また「再集録（re-registration）」とは，文学性の高いテクストは，本来は異なる種類のテクストに現れる表現様式を，新たに取り込む場合が多いことを意味します。例えば，文学性が豊富なテクストは，新聞でよく用いられている表現方法を取り込んだり，SNSのやりとりを差しはさんだり，裁判の場面で法律用語を使ったり，レストランの会話を取り入れたりするなど，多彩な表現様式を網羅しているのです。皆さんが読んだことがある文学作品をぜひ思い出してください。おそらく登場人物たちは，作品の中で新聞を読んだり，インターネットを使ったり，食事に行ったり，果ては逮捕されて裁判にかけられたりしていませんでしたか？　登場人物たちは，縦横にいろいろな場面を動き回っていたことでしょう。

　そして「多義性（polysemy）」は，例えば，一つの言葉が文字通りの意味以外

にも多くの意味を内包していることを意味します。文学らしいテクストでは，言葉が象徴的な意味で用いられることが多く，例えば，薔薇の花は，花そのものを指すだけではなく，愛や美徳，春の訪れ，時には堕落の象徴になることさえあります。言い換えれば，文学作品で用いられる言葉は，表面上の意味にとどまらず多層の意味を持ち，作品に奥行きを与えているのです。この点については，次節で改めてふれたいと思います。

二項対立を超えて

　カーターたちは，文学的言語と日常的言語を二項対立させることを批判的にとらえました。文学性を多く含むテクストと，文学性をあまり含まないテクストは，無関係ではありません。グラデーションを描くようにつながりあっていると考えたのです。彼らの主張は，近年も文体論の分野を中心に積極的に受け継がれています。

2. 児童文学が教育内容に与える利点——『幸福な王子』をめぐって

　児童文学が教育内容に与える利点を，『幸福な王子（The Happy Prince）』を例にとって考えていきましょう。前節でふれた文学らしさのうち，ここでは「多義性」と関連付けていきます。

　オスカー・ワイルド（Oscar Wilde）作『幸福な王子』は，『幸福な王子とその他の物語』として1888年に出版され，現在も読み継がれています。この作品は様々な出版社から出版されていますが，プロジェクト・グーテンベルク（Project Gutenberg）からも読むことができます。プロジェクト・グーテンベルクはインターネット上の巨大な図書館で，多彩な文学作品が登録されています。一度ぜひ，アクセスしてみてください。

いつでも「happy＝幸せ」なのか

　「How are you?」「I'm happy.」というあいさつは，小学校の英語授業では定番表現になっています。日ごろ何気なく使っている「happy」という言葉ですが，いつでも「happy＝幸せ」と解釈して良いのでしょうか。

『幸福な王子』は，若くして亡くなった王子が主人公の物語です。彼の死を悼んで，きらびやかな像が街の中心に建てられました。立派な像として生まれ変わった王子は，生前の自分の姿を振り返って，次のように言います。「My courtiers called me the Happy Prince, and happy indeed I was, if pleasure be happiness」(Wilde, 1966). 確かに自分は何不自由なく暮らしていたけれども，「快楽（pleasure）」が幸福を指すのだとしたら，「幸せ（happy）」だったかもしれないと思いを巡らすのです。ここでは「happy＝快楽」という解釈が示されています。

王子と貧しい人々

亡き王子は，街を見渡すことができる広場に置かれた立像になりました。今や王子は，貧しい人々の暮らしが手に取るように分かります。彼のところにたまたまやってきたツバメの力を借りて，サファイヤでできた自分の目や，全身を覆う金箔，装身具を飾るルビーを，人々のところに届けさせます。「happy＝贅沢を極め，自らの欲望を満たす生活」ではなく，苦しむ人々が喜ぶ姿を思い，王子は幸せを感じます。贅沢な装飾を失った王子は，最後はみすぼらしい姿になりますが，神様のもとにツバメとともに召されていきます。

作品のタイトルの意味を改めて考えるとき，「happy＝幸せ」と単純に言い切れない，意味の多層性，深さを感じることでしょう。前節でふれたように，文学作品では一つの言葉が多層の意味を持つ場合が多々あります。言葉の奥深さを感じ取る時，読者は作品を介して，作者と十分にコミュニケーションをとることが出来るのです。

表面上の意味の向こうにある意味

再び「How are you?」「I'm happy.」のやりとりに立ち返りましょう。「I'm happy.」と答えた相手は，本当に「happy＝幸せ」と思っているのでしょうか。もしかしたら疲れているかもしれない，不運なことばかりで嫌気がさしているかもしれない，それでも無理に「happy」と言っているのかもしれません。言葉の表面上の意味だけをとらえたら，相手の気持ちを十分に理解していないか

もしれない，本当の想いはすり抜けていったかもしれない――文学作品は，一つひとつの言葉には，多層の意味が含まれることを教えてくれるのです。

3. 児童文学が教育方法に与える利点――様々な媒体をめぐって

　最後に，児童文学が教育方法に与える利点を考えましょう。ここでは，挿絵やICTなどの媒体・機器を中心に，AI（artificial intelligence）時代の児童文学を考えます。

児童文学と挿絵

　児童文学において，挿絵が持つ力とはどのようなものなのでしょうか。例えばピーター・ハントは，挿絵は「第二の話（a second story）」を語る可能性があると言います（Hunt, 2001）。児童文学に関して多くの著作を残した松居直は，「子どもは挿絵に物語を読み」，眼からも物語を読み取る力を持つと主張します（松居，2003）。

　小学校4年生対象の教材『Let's Try! 2』「This is my day.」（Unit 9）を例にして，物語と挿絵の関係について考えてみましょう。この物語では，主人公が過ごすある1日の様子が描かれています。例えば，朝早くの場面では「Good morning.」という台詞が示され，「I wake up.」というト書き風の説明とともに，彼が目覚めた様子が絵で示されます。このように，主人公の生活が文字だけでなく，挿絵とともに示されていくため，子どもたちは挿絵を足場（scaffolding）にして物語の内容を理解することが可能です（文部科学省，2018）。

　挿絵が持つ意義は，足場かけに留まりません。「This is my day.」では，主人公の1日の様子とともに挿絵を通してサブストーリー（substory）が展開されています。彼の部屋にあるカレンダーに描かれた1匹の猫が絵から飛び出し，彼の後を追って学校に行ったり，公園で遊んだりする場面がさりげなく描き込まれているのです。この猫の動きに対する説明は物語本文には一切加えられていませんが，猫の動きに児童の注意を向けさせることによって，子どもたちは「猫が絵本誌面のどこにいるだろうと探し，次のページがめくられるのを楽しむ」ことが可能になると指摘されています（文部科学省，2018）。

　文字で示された内容が十分理解できない場合，挿絵の助けを借りて物語を理解することが可能です。挿絵という異なる表現手段と一体化することによって，児童文学作品を複層的に読む可能性が広がります。

児童文学と ICT

　皆さんにも思い当たることと思いますが，ゲーム機などで遊ぶ経験を積んできた子どもたちにとって，紙媒体に印刷された教材だけを使った授業は退屈に思える時もあるでしょう。GIGA スクール構想の結果，子どもたち一人ひとりがタブレットを持ち，デジタル教材が積極的に用いられるようになりました。音声を流したり，動画を映したり，電子黒板に教材を示したり，タブレットを用いて活動を行ったりするなど，ICT が様々なレベルで活用されています。

　児童文学を英語の授業で扱う際にも，ICT は威力を発揮します。例えば英語の発音に不安を持つ教師が読み聞かせを行う場合，音声や動画つきの絵本や歌教材が便利です。授業の準備段階で音声を何度も聞いて音読練習をすることができるほか，授業で既成の音声をそのまま流すこともできます。絵本の朗読だけではなく動物の鳴き声などの効果音が入った視聴覚教材を用いれば，臨場感あふれる読み聞かせも可能です。また，教材提示装置（実物投影機）があれば，絵本の細かい挿絵を大きく見せたりすることもできます。電子黒板やスクリーン上に，場面が次々に現れるデジタル教材を活用することも一案です。さらにインターネット環境が整っていれば，物語や歌・詩を扱ったホームページを用いることも考えられます。例えば，Story Online のように，俳優経験を持つ読み手が，絵本を読み聞かせる優れたページもあります。児童文学と言うと，紙に印刷された二次元の世界を思い浮かべるかもしれませんが，実際は様々な媒体・機器と相性が良いのです。

AI 時代の児童文学

　機械翻訳の機能が，驚くべき速さと精度で発展しています。AI を介せば，英語をわざわざ学習しなくても，コミュニケーションは可能だと思う人もいるかもしれません。ますます進展していくであろう AI の能力を背景にして，英

語教育における児童文学は，どのような役割を果たすのでしょうか。

　皆さんにぜひ，実験して欲しいことがあります。小学校で扱う英語会話文を，AI に翻訳させてみてください。「おはようございます」ならば「Good morning.」，「右に曲がってください」ならば「Turn right.」のように，なるほど十分すぎるほど正確に訳してくれます。一方，物語を AI に翻訳させると，おかしな英語や日本語が出てくる場合が多々あります。それはなぜでしょうか。現段階の AI は，文字が示す通りにメッセージを日本語⇔英語翻訳することは得意です。一方，物語に含まれる豊かな文脈や，多層に広がる意味内容を踏まえて，翻訳することは苦手だからです。

　私たちが目指す英語教育は，事務的に英語で用件を伝え合う能力育成ではないはずです。英語文学者として名高い外山滋比古は，「文学作品には，『わからないところ』が，日常のことばよりもより多くある」と述べて，文学の分からなさを肯定的にとらえました（外山，2002）。分かりあえないところから始まる他者との豊かな出会いのために，例え AI 全盛時代になっても，児童文学が果たす役割はますます大きくなっていくはずです。

ゆっくりの速度でふれる文学

　これまで，これからの児童文学について目を向けてきました。最後に，皆さんと児童文学の関わり方について，ふれたいと思います。

　昨今，検索エンジンを介して，インターネットから欲しい情報が瞬時に入手可能になりました。ネット上の動画は，標準速度どころか1.5倍，2倍速以上で再生できるものもあります。若い皆さんは「早送り」を好むと指摘する論評もあります（例えば，稲田，2022）。一方，優れた文学作品は，本来「瞬時」・「倍速」という概念と対極にあります。確かに作品の結末だけを知りたいのであれば，「早送り（速読）」すればよいのですが，あらすじだけが分かっても，残念ながら作品を十分に理解したとは言えません。多くの文学作品は，要件を簡潔に伝達することだけを目指していないからです。

　幸い児童文学は，短いものが多く，ゆっくりの速度でふれても長い時間は必要ありません。文学作品にふれる際は日ごろの速度を落として，作者が発する

メッセージをゆったりと受け止めたいものです。ゆっくりの速度が，私たちの慌ただしい生活にゆとりを与えてくれるかもしれません。

6　Summary & Reflection

A Summary

Here is a brief summary of the readings. Fill in the blanks to check your comprehension.

From the viewpoint of pedagogical stylistics, the language of literature is not so unique. Carter and Nash (1990) proposed six criteria for judging [1] (　　　　　) : semantic density, [2] (　　　　) dependence, displaced interaction, re-[3] (　　　　), discourse patterning, and [4] (　　　　). They emphasized that literary language should be seen as a continuous sequence of (　1　). Furthermore, literary language is not so unique, and texts conventionally regarded as non-literary can have literary qualities.

Meanwhile, children's literature can contribute to elementary school English education in terms of educational content and methods. For example, in educational content, "How are you? I'm happy." are often used in greetings without giving it much thought. However, if we use children's literature, such as *The Happy* [5] (　　　　), we can teach them that the word 'happy' has various meanings. As for educational methods, we can use multiple forms of media such as pictures, illustrations, and [6] (　　　　) tools (i.e., tablets and electronic blackboards).

Overall, children's literature has advantages for English education, especially regarding educational content and methods.

B Reflection

本章では，児童文学を英語教育で活用する観点から，文学の言葉，教育内容と教育方法上の利点について学んできました。関連する以下の語句について，

具体的な例をあげながら説明してみましょう。

	語　句	説　明
1	Pedagogical Stylistics 教育的文体論 Literariness 文学らしさ	
2	*The Happy Prince* 『幸福の王子』 Polysemy 多義性 Surface Meaning 表面上の意味	
3	Scaffolding 足場，助け Substory サブストーリー	
4	Digital Teaching Materials デジタル教材 Two-dimensional World 二次元世界 Various Media 多様な媒体	
5	Artificial Intelligence AI Literary Works and Everyday Language 文学作品と日常の言葉 Educational role of Literature in Language Teaching 言語教育における文学の教育的役割	

Unit 10
Active Learning

1 Warm-up Activities

A Choose the correct meaning for the following words or phrases using (1) to (10) below.

(　　) participate　(　　) lecture　(　　) engage　(　　) strategy

(　　) ownership　(　　) experience　(　　). motivate　(　　) authority

(　　) approach　(　　) cultivate

---

1. to attract someone's attention and keep them interested：魅了する

2. a planned series of actions for achieving something：方策

3. the fact of owning something：所有

4. to take part in an activity or event：参加する

5. to make someone want to achieve something and make them willing to work hard to do something：興味を起こさせる

6. a method of doing something or dealing with a problem：取り組み方

7. someone who knows a lot about a subject：権威

8. a long talk on a particular subject that someone gives to a group of people：講義

9. to work hard to develop a particular skill, attitude, or quality：育てる

10. knowledge or skill that you gain from doing a job or activity or the process of doing so：経験

B Read the following sentences, and check the box in front of each sentence that describes you.

☐ 1 . I have experienced a lot of discussion and pair work during lessons at school.

□ 2. I mostly listened to my teachers during lessons at school.

□ 3. It is better for us to learn something by doing it through activities.

□ 4. Activities or experiences are unnecessary to learn something in a lessons.

□ 5. I acquired English by doing activities in English lessons.

2 Aural & Oral Activities

A Read the questions below. Then listen to Track 10-1 and decide whether each sentence is True (T) or False (F) according to the conversation.

1. Rie went to see lessons in an elementary school. T/F

2. Steve was excited to see lessons at school. T/F

3. Rie saw kids trying to present during their lessons. T/F

4. Rie can imagine how to do lessons that include discussions and presentations. T/F

5. Steve thinks that active learning is important for students. T/F

B Listen again and fill in the blanks. ⌒Track 10-1 ▶

Steve : Hi, Rie. What happened? You look excited.

Rie : Hi, Steve. Yeah, I just visited an elementary school to observe some lessons.

Steve : Wow. That ¹(   ) interesting.

Rie : It was. The students had a discussion and did a presentation during the lessons. I was really surprised.

Steve : Why were you surprised? It sounds normal.

Rie : For me, it was shocking. In my schooling, I ²(   ) had any discussions, pair work or presentations.

Steve : Really. I ³(   ) had discussions and presentations.

Rie : I learned about those ⁴(   ) lectures at my university, but I couldn't imagine them at the time.

Steve : It's ⁵(   ) for us to imagine something we never experienced.

Rie :　I was lucky to observe those lessons today. Now I have to learn more about different teaching styles.

Steve : I also have to learn how to make lessons with these activities.

Rie :　We should think about lessons more in terms of ⁶(　　　　　) learning to be a better teacher.

Steve : Students need these discussion and presentation ⁷(　　　　　) in the future.

C　Let's try 'Role-Play Shadowing'.

1．Listen to the track and check the pronunciation and meaning of each word and sentence.

2．Try 'Role-Play Shadowing' using the Track with a partner.

3．Change roles and repeat.

4．Now role-play with a partner without the Track. Be sure to focus on using the appropriate intonation, rate of utterance, and tone of voice.

D　Talk with a partner, and take turns asking and answering the following questions. Then, change partners, and ask and repeat.

1．What kind of lessons did you have at your elementary school?

2．What kind of lessons did you have at your junior high school?

3．What kind of lessons did you have at your high school?

4．What kind of lessons do you like? Why?

5．What kind of lessons do you think are the most effective? Why?

3　Reading Part

A　Vocabulary and Phrases

① the learning processes　学習の過程　② teaching material　教材

③ include　含む　④ teaching methods　教授法

⑤ faculty of education　教育学部　⑥ continue　続ける

⑦ problem-solving skills 問題解決能力 ⑧ unpredictable 予測不能な
⑨ be willing to 喜んで ⑩ innovation 革新 ⑪ incorporate 取り入れる

[B] True or False Questions

Read the following statements. After you have read the passage below, answer whether the sentences are True (T) or False (F) according to the passage.

1. Active learning involves the passive participation of students. T/F

2. Active learning originally started in elementary schools. T/F

3. Active learning does not allow students to take ownership of their learning. T/F

4. Active learning is not useful for a student's future. T/F

5. Teachers using active learning must collaborate with their students to create a dynamic learning environment. T/F

[C] Multiple Choice

After you have read the passage below, circle the correct statements in each group.

1. a. Active learning strategies mean only lecture-based instructions.

   b. Active learning strategies include debate, group work, and problem-solving activities.

   c. An active learning strategy is to ask students to watch videos alone.

2. a. Active learning helps future teachers learn how to create boring and unengaging lessons.

   b. Active learning allows future teachers to be passive participants in their own education.

   c. Active learning helps future teachers learn how to create engaging and interactive lessons.

3 . a. Students are less likely to understand and retain the learning material through active learning.

　 b. Students are more likely to feel motivated and continue their learning in the future through active learning.

　 c. Students are not able to take ownership of their own learning through active learning.

4 . a. Teachers must collaborate with their students and be open to different ideas and approaches in lessons using active learning.

　 b. Teachers must be the sole authority in the classroom and not accept any input from students in lessons using active learning.

　 c. Teachers must lecture for long periods without any interaction with students in lessons using active learning.

5 . a. It is important to organize lessons and try to use many active learning strategies.

　 b. It is important to organize lessons and clarify goals for lessons.

　 c. It is important to organize lessons and give a lecture that can be understood well by students.

4　Reading Activities

🎧Track 10-2 ▶

Read the following sentences. Listen to the Track, and read it again.

Active Learning

Active learning is an approach to education that requires students to actively participate in the learning processes. Rather than simply sitting and listening to a lecture, students are encouraged to engage with the

the learning processes	学習の過程

teaching material 教材
include 含む

teaching methods 教授法

faculty of education 教育
学部

continue 続ける

problem-solving skills 問
題解決能力
unpredictable 予測不能な
incorporate 取り入れる

teaching material through a variety of different strategies. These might include discussion, group work, or brainstorming.

Active learning and its teaching methods were originally used in university education. There are many benefits to active learning, particularly for university students in a faculty of education. By using active learning strategies, future teachers can learn how to create engaging and interactive lessons that will help their own students stay motivated and interested in learning.

One of the key advantages of active learning is that it allows students to take ownership of their own learning. By participating actively in the process, students are better able to understand what they study. They are also more likely to enjoy the learning experience and feel motivated to continue learning in the future.

In addition, active learning can develop a student's problem-solving skills. In order to survive in the unpredictable society in the future, it is necessary to acquire the ability to think deeply, understand things, and find solutions. In learning that incorporates active learning, students find problems on their own and work to solve them. Students can acquire problem-solving abilities.

It may be necessary for teachers to rethink the teacher-centered approach. Rather than being the sole authority in the classroom, teachers using active learning must be willing to collaborate with their students and be open to different ideas and approaches. By doing so, they can create a dynamic learning environment that encourages creativity, innovation, and success for all students.

In the end, what is important is not simply to have classes that incorporate active learning, but to change the activities that have been discussed here based on clear goals of the kind of students the teacher wants to cultivate. It is important for teachers to think about how to design their classes with this aim in mind.

be willing to　喜んで

innovation 革新

5 Mini Lectures

1. 主体的・対話的で深い学びとは

　主体的・対話的で深い学びについて，学習指導要領総則で次の視点が挙げられています。

① 　学ぶことに興味や関心を持ち，自己のキャリア形成の方向性と関連付けながら，見通しをもって粘り強く取り組み，自己の学習活動を振り返って次につなげる「主体的な学び」が実現できているかという視点。

② 　子供同士の協働，教職員や地域の人との対話，先哲の考え方を手掛かりに考えること等を通じ，自己の考えを広げ深める「対話的な学び」が実現できているかという視点。

③ 　習得・活用・探究という学びの過程の中で，各教科等の特質に応じた「見方・考え方」を働かせながら，知識を相互に関連付けてより深く理解したり，情報を精査して考えを形成したり，問題を見いだして解決策を考えたり，思いや考えを基に創造したりすることに向かう「深い学び」が実現できているかという視点。

（小学校学習指導要領解説　総則　第3章　第3節，中学校学習指導要領解説　総則

　ここで掲げられている視点は，これらの学びの主語は「子ども」であり「子ども」がこうした学びを行うということになります。「子ども」が主体的・対話的で深い学びを実現することで，三つの柱として現行の学習指導要領で掲げられている資質・能力が身につけられるとされています。このような教育における教員の役割とは何でしょうか。

新しい学習指導要領に掲げられる育成を目指す資質・能力の三つの柱とは

　令和3（2021）年度から小学校で，令和4（2022）年度から中学校で，令和5（2023）年度から高等学校で学年進行で全面実施された学習指導要領では，全ての教科で共通して育成を目指す三つの資質・能力が示されました。

- 学んだことを人生や社会に生かそうとする，「学びに向かう力，人間性等」の涵養
- 生きて働く「知識及び技能」の習得
- 未知の状況にも対応できる「思考力，判断力，表現力等」の育成

　これらは，今回の学習指導要領の「何ができるようになるか」にあたり，柱となる考え方になります。これらの三つの要素は，既に学校教育法に学力の三要素として示されており，それらに対応するものとなっています。また，これらの三つの柱は，それぞれに独立した資質・能力ではなく，相互に関係し合いながら育成されていくものとされています。

子どもは勝手に主体的に学ぶものなのか？

　「主体的な学び」だからといって，子どもが自発的に主体的に学ぶか，というとそれはなかなか難しいことです。主体的・対話的で深い学びを実現するにも，そうした学びが実現できるように，様々な工夫を行う必要があります。このような教師主体ではない学習者主体の授業の在り方はアクティブ・ラーニン

グとして知られているものです。

　「主体的な学び」を例に見てみましょう。子どもが「主体的に学ぶ」姿として，以下のような学習者が活動の特徴があげられています（国立教育政策研究所，2020）。

・学ぶことに興味・関心を持つ
・見通しをもつ
・粘り強く取り組む
・自己のキャリア形成の方向性と関連付ける
・自己の学習活動を振り返って次につなげる

　しかし，これらのことを子どもが自ら行うということは困難であると考えられます。教師の授業改善のための様々な工夫が重要となってきます。子どもが興味・関心を持つような単元の内容や，授業の導入方法等どのようにしたら良いか，しっかりと考えることが大切になってくるのです。子どもが見通しを持てるような単元の設計，また，見通しを持てるような場面の設定や投げかけも大切になってくるでしょう。粘り強く取り組むには，教師の投げかけや発問も重要なポイントになってくるでしょう。自己の学習活動を振り返って次につなげる，ということを子ども自らが考えられるような場面の設定も必要でしょう。主体的に子どもが取り組めるような，仕掛けや場の設定などが教師の授業改善の視点としてとても重要になってくるのです。

　子どもが興味を示すような導入とはどのような導入でしょうか。教師が一方的に講義形式で話す導入で，子どもが興味を示すでしょうか。もちろん，話術に長けた教師が興味を引くように話すことで，学習題材に興味・関心を示すこともあるかもしれません。しかし，多くの場合，話を一方的に聞くだけでは興味・関心を引き出すことは難しいと考えられます。

　さて，どのようにすると興味・関心を引き出し，高めていけるのでしょうか。そこには答えはありません。そのクラス，子どもの状況により様々な方法が考えられるでしょう。これから教師を目指す学生の皆さんには，固定観念に捉わ

れず，どのような状況にも対応できるような引き出しをより多く身につけていって欲しいと思います。

　どのように教えるか，ということももちろん大切ですが，これからの時代を生きる子どもを育むためにも，どのように子どもの学びを引き出し，支えるか，という視点での授業力を身につけていくことが大切になってくるのではないでしょうか。

2.　これからの時代を生き抜く力を育むために

　主体的・対話的で深い学びの実現が求められ，子どもたちに資質・能力を身につけるのには，VUCA の時代と言われるなど，社会情勢が大きく影響しています。

VUCA とは？

　VUCA とは，新しいところでは新型コロナウイルス感染症拡大に見られるように，あらゆる事柄において未来を見通しにくくなった現代社会の状況のことを表します。もともとは，アメリカで軍事用語として使われていた言葉です。一般の社会でも従来の常識が通用しないような大きな変化が起きはじめたことから，VUCA はビジネス用語としても使われるようになり，さらに最近では教育でも注目されるようになりました。

　VUCA とは，Volatility（変動性），Uncertainty（不確実性），Complexity（複雑性），Ambiguity（曖昧性）のそれぞれ頭文字を合わせた造語になります。Volatility（変動性）とは，テクノロジーの進化や，それにともなって様々な価値観や社会の仕組みなどが変化していくことを示しています。Uncertainty（不確実性）とは，地球の温暖化による気候変動，新型コロナウイルスのような未知の疾病など，自然環境や政治，制度など未来の予測することが困難だということを示しています。Complexity（複雑性）とは，様々な要素が複雑に絡み合い，社会状況を把握しにくい状態のことを意味します。Ambiguity（曖昧性）とは，因果関係が不明で，はっきりとした正解が存在しない状況が生まれることを意味します。変動の激しい現代では，過去の実績や経験が通用せず，前例のない問題

を抱えることが増えています。

　これまでの当たり前とされていたことが，当たり前でなくなる時代を生きて
いく力を身につけていくことが必要になっていきます。

OODA ループ思考

　こうした予測困難な VUCA 時代において，その時々の状況に応じて素早く
状況判断をし，意思決定をしていく力をつけていくことも一つ求められてきま
す。

　これまで様々な分野において，PDCA サイクルをもとに継続的にその分野の
事柄の改善が進められてきました。PDCA サイクルとは，Plan（計画），Do（実
行），Check（評価），Action（改善）の頭文字をとった造語になります。しかし，
予測が困難な時代では，中長期的に，計画をして進めていく PDCA サイクル
が機能しないことも出てきました。そこで，新たに特にビジネス界で，OODA
ループと呼ばれる Observe（観察），Orient（状況判断），Decide（意思決定），Act
（行動）の頭文字を合わせた造語が生まれてきました。OODA ループ思考と呼
ばれ，現状観察から始まり，素早く意思決定されていく特徴があります。

　Observe（観察）　　：自分のまわりの状況をよく観察して変化にいち早く気づ
　　　　　　　　　　　くなど，生データを集めることを意味します。
　Orient（状況判断）：集めた生データから状況がどうなっているかを判断し，
　　　　　　　　　　　行動の方向付けを行います。
　Decide（意思決定）：状況判断に基づき，やることや計画を決め，実行に移す
　　　　　　　　　　　決定をしていきます。
　Act（行動）　　　　：やると決めたことを計画に沿って行います。そして，さ
　　　　　　　　　　　らに行動した結果どうであったか Loop（振り返る）を経
　　　　　　　　　　　て，次の Observe（観察する）へつなげていきます。

様々な状況に対応できる力

　このように VUCA の時代を生きていくには，様々な力を身につけていく必

要があると考えられます。

　このPDCAサイクルとOODAループ思考は，どちらが良い，ということではありません。それぞれが目的に応じたものになります。PDCAサイクルは，物事を継続的に改善していくためのフレームワークです。それに対し，OODAループ思考は，元々は戦場という極限状態において，瞬時に戦略的な思考や判断ができるような思考法として考えられたもので，迅速な意思決定を行う思考法なのです。PDCAサイクルはその名の通りその順序通りに展開されるのに対し，OODAループ思考は，状況に応じた適切な行動を素早く決めていくものになります。

　様々に変化していく社会の中で，目の前の物事に対して，長期的に考えていくものなのか，瞬時の判断が求められているのか，など状況に応じてどのように問題解決に向け対応していくか，と言う判断できる力であったり，またそのためにPDCAサイクルやOODAループ思考などの考え方，手段を身につけていくことであったりが，これからの時代求められてくるのではないでしょうか。

3. OECD ラーニング・コンパス（学びの羅針盤）2030

　こうした社会を取り巻く環境から教育の在り方へ影響を及ぼしてきている中，OECD（経済協力開発機構）では，2015年からOECD Future of Education and Skills 2030プロジェクト（Education 2030プロジェクト）を進めてきました。このプロジェクトは，2015年から2018年において，30を超える国から，政策立案者・研究者・校長・教師・生徒・財団・民間団体などが集まり，「2030年に望まれる社会のビジョン」と，「そのビジョンを実現する主体として求められる生徒像とコンピテンシー(資質・能力)」を共に創造・協働してきました。また，OECD諸国において，どのような生徒像や資質・能力がカリキュラムに盛り込まれているのかというカリキュラムの国際比較分析も実施してきました。

　2019年から2022年には，2015年から2018年までで検討された資質・能力の育成やカリキュラムが，現場において効果的に実施されるための手段として，カリキュラム改定と連動して改定される教授法・評価法や教員養成・教員研修などについて，引き続き，国際的な議論を重ねています。

OECD ラーニングコンパス2030

　OECD ラーニング・コンパス（学びの羅針盤）2030（以下，ラーニング・コンパス）は教育の未来に向けての望ましい未来像を描いた，進化し続ける学習の枠組みです。教育の幅広い目標を支えるとともに，私たちの望む未来，つまり個人のウェルビーイングと集団のウェルビーイングに向けた方向性を示したものになります。

　ラーニング・コンパスが提示するのは「評価の枠組み」や「カリキュラムの枠組み」ではなく，「学習の枠組み」です。この枠組みでは，生徒が2030年に活躍するために必要な資質・能力の種類に関することを幅広く提示をしています。つまりラーニング・コンパスは，大きな構造のもとで幅広い範囲と種類の学習があることを明確にし，学習そのものに価値があると示しています。学習そのものに価値があるわけですから，2030年に向けて，児童生徒が学校，家庭，そして所属しているコミュニティなど複数の層や複数の方向性で学習に参画するようになることを理解することがますます重要になってきます。

　ラーニング・コンパスの構成要素には学びの中核的な基盤，知識，スキル，態度と価値，より良い未来の創造に向けた変革を起こす資質・能力，そして見通し（Anticipation），行動（Action），振り返り（Reflection）の AAR サイクルが含まれています。

AAR サイクル

　見通し・行動・振り返り（AAR）サイクルは学習者が継続的に自らの思考を改善し，集団のウェルビーイングに向かって意図的に，また責任を持って行動するための反復的な学習プロセスです。

　計画を立てること，経験，そして振り返りを繰り返すことで学習者は理解を深め，視野を広げていくと考えられています。AAR サイクルはより良い未来の創造に向けた変革を起こす資質・能力を育成する触媒です。より良い未来の創造に向けた変革を起こす資質・能力は，学習者が状況に適応し，振り返り，必要な行動を起こし，継続して自分の考えを改善していく力に依拠しています。

6 Summary & Reflection

A Summary

Here is a brief summary of the readings. Fill in the blanks to check your comprehension.

Active learning is an approach to education that requires students to participate [1]( ) in the learning process. Active learning strategies include [2]( ), group work, and brainstorming, and they allow students to take ownership of their [3]( ) and understand the learning material deeper. It is also possible for students to acquire problem-solving skills through active learning. Students try to find a [4]( ) and solve it by themselves and with others in active learning. Students need to acquire the skills to live in an unpredictable society in the [5]( ). Thus, it is important for teachers to rethink the teacher-centered approach. However, it does not mean teachers have to try active learning in their lessons without any learning goals. It is important for teachers to set clear [6]( ) in their classes, and organize learning activities according to what kind of students they want to cultivate. Overall, active learning can be an effective method for creating a dynamic and engaging learning environment that fosters creativity, innovation, and success for all students.

B Reflection

本章では，アクティブ・ラーニングについて学んできました。アクティブ・ラーニングに関連する以下の語句について，具体的な例をあげながら説明してみましょう。

	語　句	説　明
1	Group Work グループワーク	
2	Brainstorming ブレインストーミング	
3	Unpredictable Society 予測不能な社会	
4	Ownership of their own Learning 学び責任をもつ	
5	Teacher-Centered Approach 教師中心型の指導	

Unit 11
Cooperative Learning

1 Warm-up Activities

[A] Choose the correct meaning for the following words or phrases using (1) to (10) below.

(   ) cooperation   (   ) collaboration   (   ) inquiry   (   ) assessment

(   ) ICT education   (   ) national curriculum   (   ) learning culture

(   ) project-based learning   (   ) interdependence   (   ) success criteria

---

1. a common program of education in schools：学習指導要領

2. a culture that supports independent and shared learning：学習文化

3. a group of people that depend on each other to accomplish a task：互恵性

4. learning that happens when students are engaged in a task or problem：
プロジェクト型学習

5. judging the value or quality of something：評価

6. the act of actively searching for information：探究

7. the action of working together to achieve the same goal：協力

8. the action of working together to produce something：協働

9. the standards used to judge a task or project upon completion：成功基準

10. using computers, networks, and software for learning：デジタル教育

[B] Read the following sentences, and check the box in front of each sentence that describes you.

☐ 1. I like doing group work in class.

☐ 2. I have experience doing group work in English class.

☐ 3. I have experience doing project-based learning in English class.

☐ 4. I can lead a group.

□ 5 . Collaboration is a skill I need to develop more.

2 Aural & Oral Activities

A Read the questions below. Then listen to Track 11-1 and decide whether each sentence is True（T）or False（F）according to the conversation.

1 . Rie felt he wanted to contribute more to the group. T/F

2 . Everybody got good scores though everyone did not learn. T/F

3 . Steve felt she was at fault for not designing the lesson well. T/F

4 . Every member of the group contributed using their strengths. T/F

5 . Groups must not be on the same page to work effectively. T/F

B Listen again and fill in the blanks.　　　　🎧**Track 11-1** ▶

Steve : Great presentation. How did you manage it?

Rie :　Actually, Dave and Victor did everything. No one listened to my opinion and Harry was just ¹(　　　) away.

Steve : Oh, were you able to learn the material though?

Rie :　Well, Dave and Victor already knew everything and were talking about how to get a good ²(　　　). Meanwhile, I was still trying to learn the material to join the discussion. So, I did not contribute much.

Steve : I am sorry to hear that. However, it is not entirely your ³(　　　).

Rie :　What do you mean?

Steve : Well, I mistakenly thought we all knew how to ⁴(　　　) well.

Rie :　Actually, we never learned how to do group work in school.

Steve : Thank you for bringing this to my attention. We should work on this in the next class.

Rie :　I remember my ⁵(　　　) office advisor telling me companies are saying collaboration skills are a necessary competency.

Steve : Yes. It will be one of the most important skills for you and society at ⁶(　　　). That is why I was assigned this group task.

149

Rie : Group work is fun for me. Perhaps, I was just in the wrong group.

Steve : Maybe. But I think it was more of not having a ^{7}(   ) learning goal or success criteria to follow.

C Let's try 'Role-Play Shadowing'.

1 . Listen to the Track and check the pronunciation and meaning of each word and sentence.

2 . Try 'Role-Play Shadowing' using the Track with a partner.

3 . Change roles and repeat.

4 . Now role-play with a partner without the Track. Be sure to focus on using the appropriate intonation, rate of utterance, and tone of voice.

D Talk with a partner, and take turns asking and answering the following questions. Then, change partners, and ask and repeat.

1 . Do you like doing group work?

2 . Have you ever been taught how to collaborate effectively?

3 . What kind of group work experience have you had?

4 . How much of your English class was spent on pair or group work?

5 . What is a strength you have that you can contribute to a group project?

3 Reading Part

A Vocabulary and Phrases

① cultivate 養う　② capacity 知的能力　③ competency 能力

④ inquiry 探究　⑤ assumption 推測　⑥ criteria 基準

⑦ workload 仕事量　⑧ unconventional 型にはまらない

⑨ learning evidence 学習証拠　⑩ shared-knowledge 共有知識

B True or False Questions

Read the following statements. After you have read the passage below, answer whether the sentences are True (T) or False (F) according to the passage.

1 . Collaboration is key for deep learning to occur.

2 . After learning, it is important to develop a good learning culture.

3 . It is not necessary to practice collaboration.

4 . Collaborative inquiry helps students gain knowledge and skills.

5 . Collaborative inquiry helps teachers give grades to students easily.

6 . Before collaborative inquiry, an understanding of the assessment criteria is necessary.

7 . At the end of collaborative inquiry, a letter grade or score should be given.

|C| Multiple Choice

After you have read the passage below, circle the correct statements in each group.

1 . a. The first step towards deep learning is individual study.

   b. The first step towards deep learning is group work.

   c. The first step towards deep learning is building a learning culture.

2 . a. Collaborative inquiry helps students understand what to do in the future.

   b. Collaborative inquiry helps students get a good job in the future.

   c. Collaborative inquiry helps students know more than other people.

3 . a. In collaborative inquiry, students memorize facts.

   b. In collaborative inquiry, students find their strengths.

   c. In collaborative inquiry, students build teams.

4 . a. In collaborative inquiry, students discuss learning experiences with teachers.

   b. In collaborative inquiry, students discuss learning experiences with peers.

   c. In collaborative inquiry, students reflect on their learning experiences alone.

5 . a. In collaborative inquiry, students and teachers assess learning.

   b. In collaborative inquiry, peers assess learning.

   c. In collaborative inquiry, students assess learning by themselves.

4 Reading Activities

 Track 11-2 ▶

Read the following sentences. Listen to the Track, and read it again.

Collaboration Counts

cultivate 養う
capacity 知的能力

competency 能力
inquiry 探究
assumption 推測

shared-knowledge 共有知識

Collaboration is at the heart of deep learning. However, collaboration cannot be successful until a learning culture is cultivated. Before trying to accomplish a task or project, students must develop their capacity to collaborate effectively. One way to develop this competency is through collaborative inquiry. Collaborative inquiry is a process of exploration. Students examine problems and their assumptions by engaging with others. This approach uses students' knowledge and skills to generate a shared-knowledge that is used in collaboration.

During collaborative inquiry, each student plays an important role. For instance, students identify a topic or decide on a question. They also assess their learning. As students learn through collaborative inquiry, they become experts in the learning process. This experience mirrors what students will most likely be doing in their future.

Collaborative inquiry has four phases. In Phase 1, students consider teacher expectations and establish learning goals and success criteria. In Phase 2, the learning experience is designed with students. For instance, students plan their learning which includes selecting the learning method and teams. Initially, teachers need to help students learn how to plan and collaborate effectively. Nevertheless, it saves time in future classes because students understand the learning process decreasing workload as everyone is using their strengths to make learning more effective. In Phase 3, students and teachers monitor learning and check understanding with self-reflections and learning portfolios. Thus, it is necessary to collect learning evidence during the learning process for assessment. This gradual release of learning responsibility from the teacher to the student may be unconventional at first. However, it creates a valuable learning experience as students learn to collaborate. In Phase 4, students and teachers use the collected learning evidence from formal and informal assessments and the final product to measure growth and to plan the next learning cycle.

criteria 基準

workload 仕事量

learning evidence 学習証拠

unconventional 型にはまらない

5 Mini Lectures

1. 「学び合い」

学習者中心の学びを

「授業」という言葉を聞くと，多くの人は「教壇に立つ教師が，学習者に向けて何かについて説明をしたり，質問をして学習者がその質問に答えたりする」

光景を思い浮かべることでしょう。さらに、「教師が学習者に回答の正誤を伝え、その理由を説明する」場面まで想像するかもしれません。しかしこのようなスタイルの授業では「深い学び」は成立しません。学習内容を説明していく段階で、指導者の多くは学習者が充分理解していると判断して授業を進めがちです。問題はここにあります。このような「教師主体」の授業の利点としては、学習内容を系統立てて教えられることが挙げられます。しかし、必ずしも学習者が学習内容を深く理解しているとは限りません。しっかりと学びを定着させるためには、教師は学習者の理解度を段階に応じて確認していかねばならないはずですが、どうすればよいのでしょうか。そのための一つの方法として、対話を通した「学び合い」を用いることが考えられます。学習者にとって「学び合う」ことは必要なスキルでもあり、理解や定着を促進するのに非常に効果的な方法です。教室でこの形態を導入することはさほど難しくありません。

ペア学習とグループワーク

　まずは、「二人一組のペア学習」として学び合いに慣れさせます。次に「グループ学習」につなげます。段階的に学習形態を変えていくようにします。「ペア学習」により、学習者は、教室で全員に向けて自身の意見や考えを発表する前の段階として、この心理的プレッシャーが少ない対話的な学びを通して自らの思考を深めやすくなるはずです。教師主体の授業では、たとえ教師がどんなに素晴らしい発問をしたとしても、期待する反応が得られない、全員の理解度を確認できない、といった問題を抱えたままでの進行となることが少なくありません。

　「ペア学習」を行うことで、学習者は自身の思いや考えを表現する機会を与えられ、その過程で理解が深まったり、内容の再構築が生まれたりすることにつながるはずです。また、教師は、机間指導や活動の見取りを通して理解や習得が十分にできていない学習者のための手立てを講じたり、個別指導をしたりすることができ、結果として、一人ひとりの学びを効果的に向上させることにつながるのです。

　この「ペア学習」の後に、全体に向けて発表をしたり他の学習者と意見交換

をしたりする「グループ学習」をすることで，学習者はより自信をもって発言できるはずです。その達成感から得るものが次の学習への動機づけとなり意欲的な学びへと繋がっていきます。

　具体的な手順としては，次のようになります。まず教師が発問し，その後，ペアで対話をさせます。次に，二つのペアを合体させて4人一組のグループを作り，互いの考えを交換させていきます。こうすることで，学習者は効果的な対話的学びの機会を得ることができます。最後に，全体へ向けた発表をさせ，より多くの想いや考えを共有するように進めることで，教師が一人ひとりの理解や習得を確認しながら，学習者の理解を深めていくことが可能となるのです。

効果的な学び合いを生み出すために

　この学び合いという学習形態において重要になってくるのが，学習者の学習スキルです。教師はこのスキルを効率的に身につけさせながら，その効果を確認していかねばなりません。ペアやグループにルールや役割を与えることで，学習者は様々なスキルを向上させる体験をすることが可能になります。失敗もあるでしょう。もちろん，失敗は学びの機会になり得ますが，失敗をどのように活かせば，効果的な学び合いとなるのかも含めた手立てが必要になるのです。消極的な学習者に発言をさせたり，埋没している学習者をグループの中で支援するリーダー的な役割を与えたりする等，役割を上手に与え，それぞれが学べ，学び合いが生まれる機会とすることが肝心になります。

　学び合いの学習形態を導入するにあたっては，教室での適切な「学習文化」を構築しておかなければなりません。適切な「学習文化」のある教室とは，教師と学習者が，教室で行われる活動の全てを学びにつなげようとする意識を持ち，クラスが，「自身の能力は今の段階よりもまだ伸びる」という「成長思考」を持つ「良き学びの集団」になっている教室のことです。ペアやグループ学習の際，聞き手は話し手が伝えようとしていることに真摯に耳を傾けたり，話し手は間違いや失敗を怖がらず，意見を伝えたり，互いに批評し合ったりできるのが適切な「学習文化」が醸成されている教室の特徴です。

　「学び合い」学習を導入する際には，学習効果を上げるための協働で学ぶた

めのルールとして，以下の項目を共有しておくと良いでしょう。その際，効果的に対話しているペアの様子をモデルとして紹介したり，視聴できるような動画を用意したりすることが有効です。

1．互いにしっかりと向き合う
2．はっきり，ゆっくり話す
3．尋ねられたことをしっかりと考えて答える
4．相手の発言を笑ったりしない
5．分かるまで尋ねる（聞き返すのは相手を大切にしているからこそ）
6．間違いや失敗から学ぶことを大事にする

　深い学びが起こる指導にするためには，まずは，学習者に対話的に学び合う機会を与えることが大切です。充実した学び合いが起こると，互恵効果を体験することができ，このことが，次の協働学習に効果的につながっていくことになるからです。

2．グループワークが成立するために
グループワークの弱点
　人間は一人で学習するよりも，他者と一緒にいる方が，より多くのことを学ぶ可能性があります。相手の考えを聞いたり，他者と時間や体験を共有したりすることで，学習内容をより深く学べるとする研究結果は少なくありません。これが対話的に学ぶことの意義であり，協働学習とも呼ばれるものなのです。しかし，多くの人は，グループワークを好みません。個人で学習する方がより効率的かつ効果的に学べるのだと感じている人が多いようです。その理由として，これまでなされてきたグループワークでは，「共有」と「傾聴」という二つの要素が十分になされていないからだと考えられます。

学習目標と学習規範の共有
　まず，「共有」しなければならないのは，学習目標です。つまり，ペアやグ

ループの全員が同じ学習目標を理解し，それに焦点をおきながら，学習していかなければなりません。例えば，最終的に全員が別々のワークシートを提出する課題だと，学習者の協働は必要ありません。極端に言えば，それは並行学習とも呼べます。また，一人の学習者が高得点を取るために課題に取り組み，別の学習者が練習のために同じ課題に取り組んでいれば，学習目標は「共有」されていません。教師は，学習目標を確認する機会を与える手立てを用いて学習目標から外れないように注意が向けられるように工夫するとよいでしょう。

　協働学習を成立させるには，「傾聴」する能力も必要不可欠です。互いに意見や考えを共有する重要性は言うまでもありません。注意深く聴くことは学び合いのスキルの一つなので，トレーニングを通して高めなければなりません。金森（2019）は「聴き解く力」として，「予測しながら聴く」，「反論しながら聴く」，「まとめながら聴く」，「クリティカルに聴く」等を上げ，その大切さを述べています。傾聴というスキルがあれば，学び手が建設的な批判をしたり，アイディアをシェアしたりすることで，学びの成果が高まります。

　「学習目標の共有」と「傾聴スキル」があれば，学習を「調整する能力」も育ちます。つまり，目標と照らし合わせながら効果的な学びが行われているか否かを考えることで，学習効果がさらに高まるように学びを「調整」するようになるからです。例えば，より多くの意見や考えからの相互作用を通して学ぶことを目標とすることをしっかりと理解していれば，参加している多くの人に発話の機会をバランス良く渡すターン・テイキング（発話の順序交代）が生まれるはずです。振り返り活動の際に，そのバランスが取れているかどうかに気づけるでしょう。また，単に互いにアイディアを伝え合うだけでは学びを深めることになりません。聞き手が発言者のアイディアを正確に解釈するには，当人の意見や考えの背後にある視点までも理解する必要があります。自分の考えと区別したり比較したりすることで，学習者はその内容について深く考え，深い学びへとつながるのです。

　協働学習の出来不出来は学習者の相互作用の規範と役割に依存しています。そのため，まずは規範を確立してから協働学習を実行することがポイントです。また，協働学習をうまく実践するには，年間カリキュラムや単元設計の段階か

ら計画することも肝心です。

　例えば学習者が小学生なら，次のような約束を決めることで協働学習の規範を確立することができるでしょう。

　　①課題を完了するための計画を立てて話し合いを始める（目標を考える）
　　②話者が何を伝えようとしているのかに注意を払う
　　③全員に話す機会を与える
　　④全員がどう思うか尋ねる
　　⑤意見には理由を付けて伝える

　このようにルールを簡単な動詞に置き換えて提示すれば，児童は容易に理解して行動に移すことができます。振り返り活動において誰が何回意見を出したか，どのような意見が出たかを分類してまとめるといった，学習証拠を残すような規範を作ることもできます。そうすることで，学習者は少しずつ学び合いのスキルを培っていくことが可能となるのです。

互恵依存関係が生まれる課題設定

　学び手の互恵を必要とする学習課題を設定することも重要になります。協働学習が効果的に進まないケースがありますが，その多くは，既に答えを知っている学習者が他の学習者に答えを教えることで課題を終わらせるという場合です。優れた学習課題とは，時間内に一人で完了できない課題であり，学習者同士の相互作用を必要とする課題のことです。

　例えば，「自分たちの街を ALT に紹介する」というタスク活動では，児童一人ひとりが自分のお気に入りの場所や店等を含めて，街の素敵な場所を ALT に紹介するための協働学習を行います。授業で学んだ言語材料と互いのアイディアを照らし合わせながら，「ALT の役に立つ・ALT が喜んでくれる街の紹介」を作ることになります。この活動では，一人ひとりが，自分の推しの場所や店をグループの他のメンバーに伝えるという役割を担います。英語の能力だけではなく，いろいろなアイディアを受け止め合いながら，より良い街の紹介

が完成されることになります。そこでは，グループ全員に相互依存が生じ，児童同士の互恵性も確立され，それぞれの役割を果たす責任も生まれるため，効果的な協働学習になるのです。

3.　21世紀に求められる能力

音声言語，文字言語としてのコミュニケーション能力の育成

　OECD の学習到達度調査に記述式回答が導入さるようになって，日本のランキングが低下した部分があります。日本人は一般的に，自分の意見を書いたり，表したりする自己表現への意欲が低いとみなされています。これからの言語教育において，こうした個人が自分の思いや考えを表現していくスキルの育成は，無視できない部分だと言えます。日本語や英語の授業で，「話す」，「書く」能力を身につけさせることは必須の要素となるわけです。そのためには，発信するための知識や技能の指導とともに，児童期の段階から表現する（「話す」「書く」）ことに対して積極的に取り組む態度を培うことが大切だと言えます。小学校段階から言語活動を通して自己表現をする楽しさを体験させることが重要であり，また，中学校からは，音声言語だけではなく文字言語として表現するための能力も高めたいと思えるような指導をすること，この両方が重要になってきます。

　自己表現する姿勢を効率的に身につけさせるためには何が必要でしょうか。外国語のインプットを多く与えること，外国語使用のモデルを示すこと，同時に，外国語を実際に使える十分なコミュニケーションの機会をつくることです。その際，コミュニケーションで大切となるのは相手からのフィードバックです。教師が一人で児童全員に十分なフィードバックを与えることは現実的に見て不可能と言えます。その点において，ペアやグループの仲間から多くのフィードバックがある協働学習には期待ができるはずです。

Society 5. 0に求められる教育

　一昔前の時代，仕事の現場ではマニュアルに従うことが何より重視されました。当時，就職を目指す若者には，暗記能力，正確性が要求され，教育はそれ

らの能力育成を中心になされてきました。しかし，Society 5.0にある児童には，AIと共に生きることが求められています。「不易と流行」という言葉があります。教育も時代に合わせて変化していかねばならない部分があるはずです。これからの時代，マニュアル通りの仕事は機械が受け持ちます。人間は，様々な場面において，機械やAIではなく，人間だからこそ果たせる役割を担わなければなりません。こうした需要を満たすために欠かせない能力として，コミュニケーション，コラボレーション，クリエイティビティ，クリティカル・シンキングの四つのCではじまる能力があげられます。これらの能力を身につけるためにも知識の習得は必要ですが，その知識を児童が自ら増やしていける自律的な学習者育成の助けとなる教育が求められると言えるでしょう。

　今後益々加速することになるデジタル空間と現実空間の融合された社会を生きていくにあたり，欠かせない力とは何でしょうか。それは，自分の知識不足を認める素直さ，間違いや失敗を恐れずに前へ進もうとする姿勢や態度です。学校に求められるのは，児童に間違いや失敗の体験を通して，それを乗り越える経験を与えることなのです。レジリエンスを身につけさせ，自身の取り組みを省察し，新たに解決策を創造させ，やり直しのための一歩を踏み出せる力を育てることです。さらには，自分の考えや意見を表現することに留まらず，相手の考えや意見をしっかり考え，受け止めて判断してより深い理解や新たな考えを構築する機会を持つことを通したコミュニケーション能力の育成も重要だと言えます。AI，インターネット等のICTツールを活用しながら自らの見聞を広めていく機会を充分に与えることが必要不可欠な要素と言えるのです。

プロジェクト型学習の可能性

　プロジェクト型学習や探究学習はその機会を与えてくれる学習方法です。プロジェクト型学習や探究学習は学習者が主体性を引き出し，コミュニケーション，コラボレーション，クリエイティビティ，クリティカル・シンキングの四つのCの能力を体験的に学ぶための指導法です。英語能力の正確さを目標とした指導ではなく，協働学習を通した指導においてこそ，四つのCの能力は育成されるはずであり，ICTを効果的に用いる学習体験にすることができれば，

デジタルコミュニケーション能力の育成も同時に培われることが可能となります。児童が外国語で自己表現した後，表現方法が分からない時に，自ら進んで仲間や ICT を活用してチェックする，といった自律的な学習の態度を育ててあげることできます。

　また，これからの学校教育である「令和の日本型教育」で特に注目されるのが個別最適化と協働的な学びの一体的な実現です。これはどういうことでしょうか。誰もが同じことをする，同じ方法で学ぶ，このような画一化された教育形式は，各自の個性を無視している点で優れた教育とは言い難いでしょう。教師は個々の児童が必要とするものを的確にサポートできる学習環境を構築しなければなりません。一人ひとりが必要となる知識や技能を体験的に学んでいく機会を増やしてあげることが大切になります。一方で，児童がチームで協力する大切さを学ぶことは，児童の将来の成功と結びついています。その点において，プロジェクト型学習はとても優れた方法です。活動を通して課題に遭遇し，その解決のために協働的に学びます。単独で向き合う学びとは違う，仲間との協働による学びです。ここで生まれる，学び合い，教え合いの経験こそが，生きて働く知識・技能となり，また，学習内容の深い理解につながり，今後求められる能力の育成に大きな成果をもたらすはずです。

6　Summary & Reflection

A　Summary

Here is a brief summary of the readings. Fill in the blanks to check your comprehension.

A problem the Japanese education system is facing is its ¹(　　　　　). Another problem is ²(　　　　　). We can tackle these issues by learning together. Humans in general learn more together than when they are alone. For example, by listening and sharing, we construct our understanding of something. This collaborative type of learning is called ³(　　　　　). It also helps students develop cooperation skills. Simply putting students in pairs or groups does not guarantee learning. Teachers must establish norms and roles when starting cooperative learning. Students report that they do not have enough collaborative learning experience. Thus, schools can be places students practice expressing themselves collaboratively using digital tools in a foreign language. Students cannot succeed if they are afraid of making mistakes to progress forward. If they cannot do something, they should learn how to receive help from others or solve problems in cooperation with others. One answer for schools to gain these competencies is through ⁴( ). Another form of cooperative learning is ⁵( ). These are learning approaches that provide students with the experience to explore questions or assumptions while building knowledge with other people. These approaches also provide students with the experience in developing their self-regulated learning skills to be successful in their future.

B Reflection

　本章では，言語習得（第一言語，第二言語，外国語）について学んできました。言語習得に関連する以下の語句について，具体的な例をあげながら説明してみましょう。

	語　　句	説　　明
1	Cooperative Learning 協働学習	
2	Collaborative Inquiry 協同的探究	
3	Foreign Language Education 外国語教育	

| 4 | Project-Based Learning
プロジェクト型学習 | |
| 5 | ICT Education
デジタル教育 | |

Unit 12
Language Teaching Methods

1 Warm-up Activities

A Choose the correct meaning for the following words or phrases using (1) to (10) below.

(   ) look up   (   ) entirely   (   ) real-life   (   ) improve

(   ) imitate   (   ) effective   (   ) a bit   (   ) translate

(   ) common   (   ) method

---

1. to become better than before; to make something / somebody better than before：上達する，改善する

2. a particular way of doing something：方法

3. to look for information in a dictionary：調べる

4. to express the meaning of speech or writing in a different language：翻訳する

5. producing the result that is wanted or intended; producing a successful result：効果的な

6. to copy somebody / something：まねる，手本にする

7. in every way possible; completely：全く，完全に

8. happening often; existing in large numbers or in many places：普通の

9. a little：少し

10. actually happening or existing in life, not in books, stories, or films：現実の

B Read the following sentences, and check the box in front of each sentence that describes you.

☐ 1. I do not know much about foreign language teaching methods.

☐ 2. In my high school English classes, grammar explanations and English-

Japanese translations were the main focus,

☐ 3. In my high school English classes, the teacher mostly spoke English while teaching.

☐ 4. It is desirable that English classes in Japanese elementary schools should be conducted in English.

☐ 5. I would like to learn a new foreign language entirely in that language without using Japanese.

2 Aural & Oral Activities

A Read the questions below. Then listen to Track 12-1 and decide whether each sentence is True (T) or False (F) according to the conversation.

1. Rie asked Steve for advice as to how she can improve her French. T/F

2. Steve does not think that the Grammar Translation Method is effective for adults. T/F

3. Rie is not happy if her French class is taught all in French. T/F

4. Rie has never had pair work in her French class. T/F

5. Steve believes that using the target language is more important than studying it. T/F

B Listen again and fill in the blanks.　　　　🎧Track 12-1 ▶

Rie : Hi, Steve. My French is not improving at all. You speak French [1]( ) English, so do you have any advice?

Steve : What kind of study methods do you use, Rie?

Rie : Well, I look up words in the dictionary and translate sentences using grammar. Then I memorize them.

Steve : Ah, the Grammar Translation Method. It's an effective way for [2]( ) to learn to translate a target language.

Rie : But it [3]( )help me learn to listen and speak French. Well, that may be why I don't feel like I'm improving my French.

Steve : I see.

Rie :　You said you learned French well as a child. How were you
　　　　⁴(　　　　　) ?

Steve : By listening to and imitating my French teachers. They spoke entirely
　　　　in French. That's called the Natural Approach. It's a very common teach-
　　　　ing method for children.

Rie :　I see. But if it's all in French, I'm ⁵(　　　　　) I won't understand it.

Steve : Well, it might be a bit difficult for adults. But it is important to try to use
　　　　the target language. I ⁶(　　　　　), listen to it and speak it, and then
　　　　read and write it.

Rie :　Okay. I remember ⁷(　　　　　) some pair work in my French class
　　　　too.

Steve : That kind of teaching is called Communicative Language Teaching. Stu-
　　　　dents learn the target language by using it in real-life ⁸(　　　　　).
　　　　Perhaps, you should think about using French rather than studying it.

C Let's try 'Role-Play Shadowing'.

1 . Listen to the Track and check the pronunciation and meaning of each word
　　and sentence.

2 . Try 'Role-Play Shadowing' using the Track with a partner.

3 . Change roles and repeat.

4 . Now role-play with a partner without the Track. Be sure to focus on using
　　the appropriate intonation, rate of utterance, and tone of voice.

D Talk with a partner, and take turns asking and answering the following
　　questions. Then, change partners, and ask and repeat.

1 . How were or are you taught English?

2 . Do you think the English teaching method you answered above was or is
　　effective enough?

166

3. Are you okay if your language class is conducted all in the target language?

4. Are you interested in foreign language teaching methods?

5. Do you think using the target language rather than studying it is better?

3 Reading Part

[A] Vocabulary and Phrases

① considering ～を考慮すると　② suitable 適した

③ be exposed to ～にさらされる　④ equivalent 同等の　⑤ physical 身体の

⑥ fluency 流暢さ　⑦ accuracy 正確さ　⑧ accomplish 達成する

⑨ reflect 反映する　⑩ characteristic 特徴

[B] True or False Questions

Read the following statements. After you have read the passage below, answer whether the sentences are True (T) or False (F) according to the passage.

1. The Grammar Translation Method is one option for teaching English in Japanese elementary schools. T/F

2. In the Natural Approach, teachers must be native speakers of English. T/F

3. In Total Physical Response, students are relaxed because they move their bodies without speaking English. T/F

4. In Task-based Instruction, students are encouraged to accomplish a task as quickly as possible. T/F

5. It is important to decide on one teaching method and use only that. T/F

[C] Multiple Choice

After you have read the passage below, choose the right answer to the following questions.

1. Why is the Grammar Translation Method not recommended to elementary school students?

a. They do not need grammar to learn English.

b. They do not need to translate English into Japanese.

c. They are not cognitively developed enough to understand the English grammar taught in that method.

2. In Communicative Language Teaching, what are students most encouraged to do?

a. To be careful of grammar.

b. To speak a lot even if they make mistakes.

c. To listen to their teacher's instruction carefully.

3. If you do warm-up activities in a relaxing atmosphere, which teaching method would be the best?

a. Total Physical Response

b. Task-based Language Teaching

c. Content-based Instruction

4. If you teach a home economics cooking class in English, which teaching method is recommended?

a. The Natural Approach

b. Communicative Language Teaching

c. Content and Language Integrated Learning

5. Which of the following is not mentioned in the passage?

a. It is desirable to use a combination of several teaching methods.

b. The teaching method chosen decides how well or poorly a lesson is taught.

c. Teachers should know both the advantages and disadvantages points of each teaching method.

4 Reading Activities

🎧Track 12-2 ▶

Read the following sentences. Listen to the Track, and read it again.

Language Teaching Methods

There are many different methods of teaching foreign languages, but what methods can be used to teach English in Japanese elementary schools? Considering the developmental stage of children, the Grammar Translation Method may not be suitable.

First, we will look at the two teaching methods that focus on input. In the Natural Approach, students are exposed to English, just as in first language acquisition. In this case, the teacher must have a speaking ability equivalent to that of native English speakers. They must also use English that the students can understand. In Total Physical Response, the teacher gives instructions such as 'Stand up.' in English and the children respond by moving their bodies. This method is suitable for introductory instruction and warm-up activities because it does not force the students to speak, and because it is relaxing as they move their bodies.

Next, we will look at the two methods that actively encourage students to use English. Communicative Language Teaching involves activities such as pair work, group work, and role play. In these activities, priority is given to fluency rather than to accuracy. In Task-based Language Teaching, students work in

Grammar Translation Method 文法訳読法

suitable 適した

be exposed to English 英語にさらされる

equivalent 同等の

Total Physical Response 全身反応指導法

fluency 流暢さ

accuracy 正確さ

Task-based Language Teaching タスク中心指導法

accomplish 達成する
reflect 反映する

pairs or groups to accomplish tasks in English. These tasks should reflect real-world language use and provide a sense of accomplishment and enjoyment from working together with friends.

Finally, we will look at the two teaching methods that deal with the content of other subjects. In Content-based Instruction, content from other subjects, such as science and social studies, is taught in English. The student's attention needs to be focused on the subject content rather than on the target language. A similar teaching method is Content and Language Integrated Learning. While the former has been practiced in North America, the latter has become popular mainly in Europe.

In conclusion, it is important to understand the characteristics of each of these teaching methods and to use them in combination according to the learner's situation and teaching goals.

deal with ～を扱う
Content-based Instruction
内容中心教授法

Content and Language
Integrated Learning 内容
言語統合型学習

characteristics 特徴
in combination 組み合わ
せて

5 Mini Lectures

1. ナチュラル・アプローチと全身反応指導法
小学校英語教育で活用できる外国語教授法

　外国語教授法にはいろいろなものがあります。例えば，日本の中学校や高等学校の英語の授業で従来よく用いられた教授法には文法訳読式 (Grammar Translation Method) があります。この教授法では，教師は学習者の母語を使って演繹的に文法規則を教え，学習者はそれらを暗記してドリル練習と翻訳に取り組みます。一方，リスニングやスピーキングの練習は行われません。したがって，効率的に読解力を育成することは可能ですが，リスニングやスピーキングの能力は身につきません。このことから，リスニングとスピーキングが中心となる

小学校英語の授業場面において，抽象的・論理的思考能力が十分に発達していない学齢の児童を対象とした教授法としては適していないと言えます。

　では，小学校外国語活動・外国語の授業で活用できる教授法にはどのようなものがあるでしょうか。本章の Mini Lecture では，３回に分けて二つずつの教授法を紹介していきます。教授法はどれか一つを選択するというよりも，学習者の状況や指導目標に合ったものを選択して組み合わせて活用することが大切なので，それぞれの教授法の特徴をよく理解しましょう。

ナチュラル・アプローチ

　ナチュラル・アプローチ（The Natural Approach）とは，子どもが母語を習得するように自然に第二言語も習得すべきであるとする指導法で，目標言語によるインプットが重視されます。スティーヴン・クラッシェン（Stephen Krashen）のインプット仮説（Input Hypothesis）を理論的背景とし，理解可能なインプット（comprehensible input）を十分に受けることによって，自然な言語習得が起きると考えられています（Krashen & Tereell, 1983）。その際，学習者の不安や学習意欲の欠如，自信喪失などの心理的な問題がフィルター（障壁）となり，インプットが学習者の中に入りにくくなるとされ（情意フィルター仮説：Affective Filter Hypothesis），学習者の不安を和らげる，つまり，情意フィルターを低くするような配慮が必要とされています。また，この教授法では，教師が目標言語の母語話者であるか，母語話者と同等のスピーキング能力がある必要がありますが，その場合も，学習者が理解できるようなティーチャートークを行わなければなりません。

　では，具体的な小学校英語の授業場面を見てみましょう。ALT がナチュラル・アプローチを用いて，児童に大量のインプットを与えています。一緒にティームティーチングをしている担任も英語を多用していますが，児童が理解できていない，または不安そうにしていると判断したときには，さりげなく日本語での説明や励ましの言葉を付け加えています。これは，児童の情意フィルターを下げてインプットを受け入れやすくしているのです。

全身反応指導法

　全身反応指導法（Total Physical Response：TPR）とは，ナチュラル・アプローチと同様に子どもの母語習得をモデルとした教授法で，教師の目標言語による指示に対して学習者が身体で反応する活動を通して言葉を習得させる教授法です。リスニングのみに焦点が置かれていて発話を強制しないことや，身体を動かすことによって緊張がとけることが，外国語学習の入門期や特に低年齢の子どもの教授法として適していると言われています。リスニング以外の技能への配慮があまりないことや，動作と結びつかない表現は扱いにくいという課題から，中・上級者には適さないという指摘もありますが，小学校の英語の授業でよく使用されている教授法です。

　では，具体的な授業場面を見てみましょう。外国語活動の時間に，サイモン・セズ（Simon Says）のゲームをしています。教師が「Simon says, "Stand up."」と言ったら，児童はみんな立ち上がります。続いて，教師が「Sit down.」と言うと，ほとんどの児童はそのままですが，数人の児童が座りました。このゲームでは，文頭に「Simon says」と言われたときのみ，その指示通りに動作するというルール（サイモンは王様なので，王様が言ったときだけ，その動作をする）なので，今回座った児童は間違ったことになり，1回休むなどのルールを決めておきます。教師は，児童が理解でき，教室内でできる動作の表現(例：Turn right /left. Raise your hand. Put your hand down.) を集めておいて，次々に発話していきます。サイモン・セズ以外の活用例としては，指示を聞いてカードを並べ替えたり，色を塗ったりなどの多様な活動もでき，授業のウォームアップ活動として，既習の表現を使って TPR を行うことも可能です。

2. コミュニカティブ・ランゲージ・ティーチングとタスク中心教授法
コミュニカティブ・ランゲージ・ティーチング

　コミュニカティブ・ランゲージ・ティーチング（Communicative Language Teaching：CLT）とは，コミュニケーション能力（communicative competence）の養成を目標とした教授法の総称であり，コミュニカティブ・アプローチ（Communicative Approach）とも呼ばれます。学習者に目標言語を積極的に使用させ

ることを授業の中心とし，その際，正確さ（accuracy）よりも流暢さ（fluency）を重視します。言い換えると，文法的な間違いがあっても，たくさん発話しながら意味のやりとりをすることを優先します。したがって，文法などの文構造に関わる知識の習得それ自体を学習対象の中心にすることはありません。この教授法は，現在，世界で広く受け入れられている指導法の一つですが，コミュニケーション能力そのものの明確な記述が完成していないことや，文法指導が軽視され過ぎることがあるなどの課題も指摘されています（白畑ほか，2019）。

　では，小学校の英語の授業での具体的な活用例を見てみましょう。この教授法では，状況や文脈を明確にして，ペアワークやグループワーク，ロールプレイなどの活動を多用します。あるペアワークでは，児童がそれぞれ異なる動物園の地図を持っていて，「Do you have lions?」「Yes, I do. I have two lions.」などと言ってお互いの動物園にいる動物を確認し合っています。このように自分の持っている情報と相手が持っている情報にずれ（information gap）があるときにはコミュニケーションする必然性が生まれるので，児童は英語を聞いたり話したりする活動に自然に参加することができます。このような活動を，インフォメーション・ギャップ活動（information-gap task）と呼びます。また，教師の役割は基本的にはコミュニケーションを促進させる補助役なので，児童の英語の誤りを正すことに焦点が置かれることはありません。この教授法では，児童が実際に英語を使ってコミュニケーションする楽しさを味わうことができるので，児童の興味・関心や学習段階に合った活動を設定して，積極的に活用したい教授法と言えるでしょう。

タスク中心教授法

　タスク中心教授法（Task-based Language Teaching：TBLT）のタスク（task）とは言語習得を目的として行う課題や作業のことで，この教授法では学習者のニーズに基づいてタスクを選定し，タスクを遂行するために目標言語で積極的に相互交流（interaction）する機会を学習者に与え，教室内で意味を伝え合おうとする双方向の努力（意味交渉）を活発に行わせます。この相互交流の中で意思の疎通に支障が出た場合，対話者はお互いに言葉を修正したり，修正を求め

たりして，意味を伝え合おうと努力します。その結果，学習者に理解可能なインプット（comprehensible input）や，相手からのフィードバック（feedback），およびアウトプットする機会などを与えるため，第二言語習得が促進されると考えられています。タスクの実行に際しては，グループワークやペアワークが用いられることが一般的で，タスクは現実社会での言語使用を反映したものが望ましく，相互交流では英語の正確さよりも意味伝達に焦点が置かれます。そのため，文法指導が軽視されるという課題も指摘されています。

　では，小学校の外国語科の授業での活用例を見てみましょう。家庭科で栄養素（炭水化物，脂質，たんぱく質，ミネラル，ビタミン）について学習したことを活用し，栄養バランスが良く，費用も安く抑えることができるオリジナル・ピザをグループで考え，材料を買い，できたピザをクラスで発表するというタスクを設定します。児童は，材料の語彙(tomato, potato, green pepper, sausage, bacon, tuna, cheese, egg, olive oil など) や買い物に必要な表現（What would you like? / I'd like～. How much is it? / It's ～ yen. など）を学習します。そして，オリジナル・ピザを考えて買い物をするグループとお店役のグループを複数作るとともに，おおまかな予算と現実的な値段設定（ただし，値段の交渉は可能とします）をしておき，材料やお金の絵カードを準備します。タスクを実行する前には，具体的なやりとりをデモンストレーションして見せ，どの児童も自信をもって取り組めるようにします。また，特定の児童に頼るのではなく，グループ全体で協力することが大切であることを確認しておきます。このように，友達と協力してタスクをやり遂げる楽しさや達成感を得ることができることもタスク中心教授法の利点と言えるでしょう。

3. 内容中心教授法と内容言語統合型学習
内容中心教授法

　内容中心教授法（Content-based Instruction：CBI）とは，目標言語を用いて理科，社会などの教科の内容（content）や環境問題などの特定テーマの内容を学習者に教え，その過程において目標言語を自然な形で習得させようという教授法で，Content-based Approach とも呼ばれます。これは，私たちの実際のコミュ

ニケーションでは，言語は考えや情報等の「内容」を伝えたり，理解したりする道具として働いているので，第二言語の指導においても内容の伝達を重視しようとする考え方に基づいています。

　CBIにはイマージョン・プログラム（immersion program）のように学校での教科学習の多くを目標言語で行うものから，外国語の授業において内容を重視したトピックを設定して目標言語で授業を行うものまで，幅広いレベルでの活用方法があります。前者の例を挙げれば，日本の学校で国語の授業以外の全教科を英語で行うトータル・イマージョンや，一部の教科を英語で行うパーシャル・イマージョンがあります。いずれの場合も，教師が扱う内容について熟知している必要があり，英語と当該教科の両方に精通している教師を確保することが容易ではないという課題があります。また，言語形式よりも内容に重点が置かれるため，文法能力の伸長はあまり期待できないという指摘もあります。

　一方で，小学校学習指導要領の外国語科　第2　各言語の目標及び内容等には，「オ　言語活動で扱う題材は，（中略），国語科や音楽科，図画工作科など，他の教科等で児童が学習したことを活用したり，学校行事で扱う内容と関連付けたりするなどの工夫をすること。」との記述があり，同解説書で他教科等の学習の成果を外国語科の学習の中で適切に生かすことが推奨されています。小学校英語ではCBIとして他教科の新しい学習内容を扱うことは現実的ではありませんが，CBIを広義に捉えて，他教科での成果や既習の学習内容を復習として取り上げるCBI的な授業実践は可能でしょう。

　では，小学校英語教育でのCBI的な活動例を見てみましょう。社会科では食料の輸入先を調べて発表する活動（表現例：Pork comes from America.），算数科では加減乗除（表現例：Three plus five is eight. Nine minus two is seven.），そして理科では食物連鎖（food chain）を扱うことができます。食物連鎖の指導の手順としては，まず，plant, nut, grasshopper, frog, squirrel, rabbit, fox, bird, eagleなどの語彙を導入します。その後，「Which eats which?」と問いかけることによって，児童から様々な答えが返ってくるでしょう。その答えをつないでいくと，Rabbits eat plants. Eagles eat rabbits. のように三つを結ぶ短いものから，Squirrels eat nuts. Foxes eat squirrels. Eagles eat foxes. のように四つを結ぶも

のや，Grasshoppers eat plants. Frogs eat grasshoppers. Birds eat grasshoppers. Eagles eat foxes. のように五つを結ぶ食物連鎖が出来上がります。この過程で，児童は英語の語順 SVO とこれらの語彙を学習しているというよりも，食物連鎖という教科内容に注意が向いています。

内容言語統合型学習

　内容言語統合型学習（Content and Language Integrated Learning：CLIL）は，教科等の内容（content）の学習と外国語という言語（language）の学習を統合して（integrate）行う学習であり，内容と言語を統合的に教える点では前述の CBI と共通している指導法です。CBI が北米の ESL 環境で実践されてきたのに対し，CLIL はヨーロッパの EFL 環境において非ネイティブ教師の指導によって普及したという相違点があります。CLIL の詳細については Unit 14 で扱うので，ここでは簡潔に説明します。その主な特徴は，四つの C（4Cs）と呼ばれている四つの軸，つまり，内容（Content），言語（Communication），認知（Cognition），文化（Culture / Community）が存在することです。具体的には，内容（Content）と言語（Communication）を統合しながら学習を進めていきますが，その際に，学習者が考えたり，分析したり，振り返ったり，知識を応用したりする認知活動（Cognition）や文化理解を促す学習（Culture / Community）も行い，これらの四つをセットとして授業実践を行います。

　では，小学校での具体的な活用例を見てみましょう。家庭科の時間にカレーライス（curry and rice）の調理実習をした後に，外国語の授業で ALT と一緒に調理をします。ALT と一緒に作ることにより，英語を使う必然性が生じます。また，カレー自体はインドが発祥地ですが，その後イギリスに渡り，明治時代に日本に入ってきて現在私たちが食べているカレーライスができたという経緯から，カレーライスは異文化理解の中の文化交流の観点からも興味深い題材であり，児童の多様な思考を促すことが可能です。

6 Summary & Reflection

A Summary

Here is a brief summary of the readings. Fill in the blanks to check your comprehension.

When teaching foreign languages in Japanese elementary schools, the
¹(   ) of the different methods should be examined.

First, the Natural Approach and Total ²(   ) Response (TPR) focus on ³(   ). In the Natural Approach, students are exposed to English through comprehensible input by the teachers and other resources. In TPR, the teacher gives orders in English and the children respond by moving their bodies. TPR is suitable for warm-up activities because it is relaxing as they move their bodies.

Next, ⁴(   ) Language Teaching (CLT) and Task-based Language Teaching (TBLT) actively encourage students to use English. In CLT,
⁵(   ) is regarded as more important than accuracy during students' pair or group work. In TBLT, students work together to accomplish tasks in English.

Finally, Content-based Instruction (CBI) and Content and Language
⁶(   ) Learning (CLIL) deal with the content of other subjects. In CBI, content from other subjects is taught in English. CBI has been practiced in North America, while CLIL has become popular in Europe.

To conclude, teachers should remember these characteristics of teaching methods and use them in ⁷(   ) considering the learner's situation and teaching goals.

B Reflection

本章では，外国語教授法について学んできました。小学校英語教育で活用できる六つの外国語教授法について，具体的な活動例をあげながら説明してみま

しょう。

	語　句	説　明
1	Natural Approach ナチュラル・アプローチ	
2	Total Physical Response ：TPR 全身反応指導法	
3	Communicative Language Teaching ：CLT コミュニカティブ・ラン ゲージ・ティーチング	
4	Task-Based Language Teaching：TBLT タスク中心教授法	
5	Content-Based Instruction：CBI 内容中心教授法	
6	Content and Language Integrated Learning： CLIL 内容言語統合型学習	

Unit 13
ICT Education

1 Warm-up Activities

A Choose the correct meaning for the following words or phrases using (1) to (10) below.

(   ) national   (   ) brilliant   (   ) device   (   ) communication

(   ) technology   (   ) group   (   ) environment   (   ) interactive

(   ) literacy   (   ) database

---

1. the process by which people exchange information or express their thoughts and feelings：コミュニケーション

2. relating to a nation：国家の

3. several people or things that are all together in the same place：集団

4. a large amount of data stored in a computer system so that you can find and use it easily：データベース

5. the people and things that are around you in your life：環境

6. the state of being able to read and write：リテラシー

7. a machine or tool that does a special job：機器

8. very successful：輝いた

9. involving talking and working together：相互に影響しあう

10. new machines, equipment, and ways of doing things that are based on modern knowledge about science and computers：テクノロジー

B Read the following sentences, and check the box in front of each sentence that describes you.

☐ 1. I have my own computer.

☐ 2. I use a tablet computer more often than I use a desktop computer.

☐ 3 . I think that a computer is more useful than a tablet computer.

☐ 4 . I have used ICT devices in lessons at school.

☐ 5 . I am good at doing things such as writing reports, calculating numbers using a digital devices.

2 Aural & Oral Activities

[A] Read the questions below. Then, listen to Tarck 13-1 and decide whether each sentence is True (T) or False (F) according to the conversation.

1 . Rie is good at using a computer. T/F

2 . Steve is used to using computers. T/F

3 . Rie has used computers at school before. T/F

4 . In Japan, every student has a computer now. T/F

5 . Rie will learn how to use a computer at school for her future. T/F

[B] Listen again and fill in the blanks.　　　🎧Track 13-1 ▶

Rie :　Steve. I need your ¹(　　　　).

Steve : What happened, Rie?

Rie :　I'm making a presentation for one of my lessons, but I'm not good at using computers.

Steve : OK. Let me see.

Rie :　Thank you. Wow, you are amazing. How did you get ²(　　　　) computer skills?

Steve : At school. I ³(　　　　) used computers in my lessons to research write essays, and make presentations.

Rie :　That ⁴(　　　　) nice. So you got used to using computers then.

Steve : Yeah. Did you use a computer at school?

Rie :　Sometimes. But I just practiced ⁵(　　　　).

Steve : I see. Now in Japan, each student has a computer in their lessons, right?

Rie :　Using computers at school has ⁶(　　　　) promoted since 2020. I have to learn how to use one for my lessons if I want to be a teacher.

Steve : Me, too! Let's work ⁷(　　　　　) on that!

[C] Let's try 'Role-Play Shadowing'.

1. Listen to the Track and check the pronunciation and meaning of each word and sentence.

2. Try 'Role-Play Shadowing' using the Track with a partner.

3. Change roles and repeat.

4. Now role-play with a partner without the Track. Be sure to focus on using the appropriate intonation, rate of utterance, and tone of voice.

[D] Talk with a partner, and take turns asking and answering the following questions. Then, change partners, and ask and repeat.

1. What ICT device do you own?

2. What ICT device do you often use in your daily life?

3. Have you ever taken lessons using a computer at school?

4. What can you do using a computer?

5. How do you learn with your smartphone?

3 Reading Part

[A] Vocabulary and Phrases

① refer 紹介する　② Course of Study 学習指導要領　③ promote 推進する
④ a wider range of より広い範囲　⑤ equip 能力を養う　⑥ solving 解決する
⑦ status-quo 現状（維持），そのままの状態　⑧ despite 〜にもかかわらず
⑨ inequalities 不平等　⑩ qualified 適性のある　⑪ integrate 統合する
⑫ overall 全般的に言えば

[B] True or False Questions

Read the following statements. After you have read the passage below, answer whether the sentences are True (T) or False (F) according to the passage.

1 . Japanese students begin learning about ICT at a young age. T/F

2 . ICT education in Japan focuses only on teaching students how to use technology. T/F

3 . The goal of ICT education in Japan is to prepare students for their future. T/F

4 . ICT education in Japan does not involve any group projects. T/F

5 . All schools in Japan have equal access to technology and resources for ICT education. T/F

C Multiple Choice

After you have read the passage below, circle the correct statements in each group.

1 . a. 'ICT' stands for International Commerce Trade

b. 'ICT' stands for Information and Computer Technology

c. 'ICT' stands for Information and Communication Technology.

2 . a. Children in Japan start learning about programming from junior high school.

b. Children in Japan start learning about programming from high school.

c. Children in Japan start learning about programming from elementary school.

3 . a. One of the goals of ICT education in Japan is to prepare students for Society 5.0.

b. One of the goals of ICT education in Japan is to teach students traditional subjects like math and science.

c. One of the goals of ICT education in Japan is to encourage students to pursue careers in the arts.

4 . a. An important aspect of ICT education in Japan focuses on competition and individual achievement.

b. An important aspect of ICT education in Japan is a focus on collaboration and working together.

c. It is important from the perspective of ICT education in Japan to focus on memorization and repetition.

5 . a. There are inequalities in educational opportunities due to an uneven access of technology and resources.

b. All schools have equal access to technology and resources.

c. There is no need for more qualified ICT teachers.

4 Reading Activities 　🎧**Track 13-2** ▶

Read the following sentences. Listen to the Track, and read it again.

ICT Education

    ICT stands for Information and Communication Technologies. In recent years, ICT education in Japan refers to the use of digital technology to access, process, and communicate information. It is written in the Course of Study. Now it is being promoted in initiatives such as the National GIGA School Plan.

    ICT education in Japan starts at a young age, with students learning programing skills and information literacy in elementary school. As students progress through junior and high school, they have access to a wider range of ICT tools and resources, including networks and databases.

refer 言及する

Course of Study 学習指導要領

promote 促進する

a wider range of より広い範囲

One of the goals of ICT education in Japan is to prepare students for Society 5.0. It aims to equip students with ICT skills and knowledge needed to use and create digital technology. Thus, students will be better positioned to succeed in a better society while contributing to the economy and solving social issues.

Another important aspect of ICT education in Japan is to create a better learning environment for each student. Through group projects, students learn how to work effectively with others and how to apply their ICT skills to real-world challenges. Even in a class of about 40 students. ICT can also support individual learning in line with each student's needs and situation. In other words, ICT has potential to change the status-quo of lessons in Japan. Despite the many benefits of ICT education in Japan, there are also many problems that need to be considered. For example, not all schools have the same level of access to technology and resources, which can create inequalities in educational opportunities. In addition, there is a need for more qualified ICT teachers who can effectively integrate digital technology into their teaching.

Overall, ICT education in Japan is a dynamic and rapidly progressing field that holds great promise for the students' futures. By continuing to invest in this area, teachers can help to ensure that Japanese students are well-prepared for the digital age and the opportunities and challenges it presents.

equip 能力を養う

solving 解決する

status-quo 現状（維持），そのままの状態
despite 〜にもかかわらず

inequalities 不平等
qualified 適性のある
integrate 統合する

overall 全般的に言えば

5 Mini Lectures

1. 日本の ICT 教育の歴史と現状

これまでの ICT に関連した教育

　ここ数年急速に学校現場での ICT 環境の整備が進み，ICT 教育が推進されている印象を受けますが，これまで各教科の指導において視聴覚教育機器を利用した指導は行われていますし，また，情報教育として取り組まれてきています。

　平成元 (1989) 年告示の学習指導要領では，中学校技術・家庭科において，選択領域として「情報基礎」が新設され，中学校・高等学校段階で，関連する各教科で情報に関する内容が取り入れられるとともに，各教科の指導において教育機器を活用することとされました。

　平成10 (1998) 年12月に小学校及び中学校学習指導要領が改訂，公示されました (高等学校学習指導要領は平成11年3月告示)。この学習指導要領では，小・中・高等学校段階を通じて，各教科や総合的な学習の時間においてコンピュータや情報通信ネットワークの積極的な活用を図るとともに，中学校・高等学校段階において，情報に関する教科・内容を必修とするなど，情報教育の充実を図りました。具体的には，中学校技術・家庭科技術分野で「情報とコンピュータ」を必修 (発展的な内容は生徒の興味・関心に応じて選択的に履修) とするとともに，高等学校で普通教科「情報」を新設し必履修とし，専門教科「情報」を新設しました (11科目で構成)。

　平成20 (2008) 年3月，小学校及び中学校の学習指導要領が改訂公示され，教育の情報化について，情報教育及び教科指導における ICT 活用の両面で様々な充実が図られました。また，平成21 (2009) 年3月には，高等学校及び特別支援学校の学習指導要領が改訂公示され，小学校・中学校と同様に情報教育及び教科指導における ICT 活用について様々な充実が図られました。

　平成29 (2017) 年3月に小学校及び中学校の学習指導要領が，同年4月に特別支援学校小学部・中学部の学習指導要領が改訂公示され，「情報活用能力」を言語能力等と同様に「学習の基盤となる資質・能力」と位置付け，その育成を図るために，「各教科等の特質を生かし，教科等横断的な視点から教育課程の編成を図る」こととされ，また，情報活用能力の育成を図るため，各学校に

おいて ICT 環境を整備し，これらを適切に活用した学習活動の充実を図ることとされました（小学校学習指導要領（平成29年告示）第1章　第2，中学校学習指導要領（平成29年告示）第1章　第2　高等学校学習指導要領（平成30年告示）第1章　第2款）。

　併せて，小学校及び特別支援学校小学部の学習指導要領において ICT の基本的な操作を習得するための学習活動及びプログラミング教育を各教科の特質に応じて計画的に実施することとされたことをはじめ，各学習指導要領において情報教育及び教科指導における ICT 活用の両面で様々な充実が図られました。平成30（2018）年3月に改訂告示された高等学校学習指導要領及び平成31（2019）年2月に改訂告示された特別支援学校高等部学習指導要領においても，小・中学校と同様に「情報活用能力の育成」や ICT 環境の整備等について記載がされ，高等学校においても「情報Ⅰ」が必履修科目として新設されるなど情報教育及び教科指導における ICT 活用について様々な充実が図られました。

日本の ICT 教育の現状

　学習指導要領で，長らく ICT 関連の学習活動の内容が記載されていたにもかかわらず，実際のところその環境整備などが進まない現状がありました。

　文部科学省が実施する「令和元年度学校における教育の情報化の実態等に関する調査」によれば，第3期教育振興基本計画に定めた学習者用コンピュータの整備目標値が3人に一台とされているにもかかわらず，全国平均値は4.9人に一台にとどまったままであり，地域間による差も大きく見受けられました。

　また，2018年に行われた OECD 生徒の学習到達度調査(Programme for International Student Assessment : PISA) によると，授業におけるデジタル機器の使用率は OECD 加盟国の中で最下位という結果でした。数学を例にとると，数学の授業で ICT 機器を利用しないと回答した割合は，OECD 加盟国全体で54.4％なのに対し，日本は89.0％となっています。ICT 機器を単に利用すれば良いということではありませんが，その違いは大きいものであることが分かります。

GIGA スクール構想

　そうした状況を危機に感じ，国による ICT 教育の推進が一層進められるようになり，「GIGA スクール構想」が本格化されるようになりました。「GIGAスクール構想」とは，以下の二つを柱に，全国の各学校で進められている ICT教育環境の整備を通した教育充実計画のことです（文部科学省, 2020）。

- ・1人1台端末と，高速大容量の通信ネットワークを一体的に整備することで，特別な支援を必要とする子供を含め，多様な子供たちを誰一人取り残すことなく，公正に個別最適化され，資質・能力が一層確実に育成できる教育 ICT 環境を実現する
- ・これまでの我が国の教育実践と最先端の ICT のベストミックスを図ることにより，教師・児童生徒の力を最大限に引き出す

2.　英語教育と ICT

　「GICA スクール構想」の後押しを受けて，日本の ICT 教育は，急速に進んでいます。実は，英語教育分野においては，視聴覚機器を用いた教育の実践に長い歴史があります。特に音声指導に関しては，古くはソノシートやレコード盤用の蓄音機，テープレコーダ，カセットテープレコーダ，CD プレイヤー，MD プレイヤー等，また，スライド，OHP(オーバーヘッドプロジェクター)，OHC（オーバーヘッドカムシャフト／書画カメラ）等の多くの視聴覚機器が教室で使われてきていました。映画などの映像を活用した授業も行われてきており，映像再生機器も多くの授業で使用されてきています。タイピングの練習も兼ねて，PC ルームなどでライティングを行なったり，スピーチや会話を録音し聞き直したりするなどの活動を行なう授業もありました。

　高等学校などには，LL 教室（Language Laboratory）や CALL 教室（Computer Assisted Language Learning），といった，PC を始めとした ICT 機器を揃えた英語の授業用の教室を設置しているところもありました。

　このように，ICT 機器を活用した英語の授業が繰り広げてきていたわけでが，一人一台端末が整備された現在，その授業の在り方も大きく様変わりしようと

しています。

ICT 機器によって変わる英語教育

　一人一台端末が整備されたことにより，外国語学習において重要な役割を果たす個々の能力や目的に応じた音声教材を用いた学びの実施が容易になってきています。

　例えば，音読練習の場面です。これまで皆で音声を聞いたり，その後，練習したりという活動が展開されてきました。練習をしている最中に音声がよく分からない，という時に，教師に質問するなどするしか確認する方法がありませんでした。多くの生徒が質問してしまうと，きちんと確認できないまま音読の時間が終わってしまう，ということも多々ありました。しかし，一人一台の端末が導入されたことで，教科書には QR コードなどから簡単に音声教材にアクセスできるようになっており，学習者のニーズに応じて活用することが可能になっています。こうしたことから，教室では，音読の個人練習の時などに，音声教材を利用して様々なスピードでシャドーイングをしている生徒や発音のモデルを聞いて確認している生徒，自身の発音を発音矯正ソフトウエアでチェックしている生徒等，様々な使用が見受けられるようになりました。

　録音機能を利用することで，教科書本文の音読など容易に録音することができるようになり，学習者が自分の発音を確認，改善していくこともできるようになっています。これまでは，一人ひとりの生徒の音読の様子を確認しようとすると，授業時間が大幅に裂かれるなどのことからあまり行われてきませんでしたが，実施のためのハードルが下がり教師側の負担も軽減されることになりました。

　音声入力による文書作成ソフトを利用した指導では，教科書本文などを音読することで，自動的に入力がなされ，文字となって打ち出されます。つまり，認識される発音が身についているかどうかの判定がすぐに分かようになっているわけです。音声認識機能における誤差も少なくなってきているので，この機能を使うことで，学習者自身で通じる発音を意識しながら音読練習をすることが可能となっています。

　また，これまで ALT（Assistant Language Teacher）が教科担当や担任と一緒に授業が行われてきました。授業で身につけた英語を実際に使う場面として，児童生徒のコミュニケーション能力の育成の一助となってきました。一人一台端末が整備された現在，画面越しに，海外の方々や姉妹校等の同じ学年の子どもたちと一対一で，英語でコミュニケーションを図る機会を得ることも起こっています。例え数十分の間でも，一対一であったり，状況によっては，2～3人の児童生徒に対して一人のネイティブ・スピーカーがいたりすることで，自分達の等身大の英語で工夫をしてコミュニケーションを図ろうとする姿が見られ，また，楽しみながら取り組んでいる様子が見受けられます。このような直接的な対話の体験は，画面越しであっても，普段の英語の授業で身につけた知識や技能を実際の場面で目的を持ち活用する機会となり，大変意義のあることです。一人一台端末が導入されたことで，児童生徒の英語の活用場面の選択肢が広がったことは間違いないでしょう。

3. 学校における ICT の活用の実際
教科に関する ICT 活用

　ICT 機器の活用は，教科の指導に留まらず，学校において様々な活用が考えられます。

　教科に関する ICT 活用としては，まず，デジタル教科書の使用があげられます。デジタル教科書は，二つのタイプに分かれます。一つが，指導者用デジタル教科書でもう一つは学習者用デジタル教科書です。

　学習者用デジタル教科書について，国は，平成30（2018）年に学校教育法第三十四条の一部を改正する法律で「紙の教科書の内容を文部科学大臣の定めるところにより記録した電磁的記録（中略）である教材（学習者用デジタル教科書）がある場合には，文部科学大臣の定めるところにより，児童の教育の充実を図るため必要があると認められる教育課程の一部において，紙の教科書に代えて学習者用デジタル教科書を使用できる。」と定めました。このことにより，紙ベースの教科書に加え，必要に応じて学習者用デジタル教科書を併用することができるようになったわけです（文部科学省，2018）。

この学習者用デジタル教科書は，紙ベースと同一の内容がデジタル化されたものであり，指導者用のデジタル教科書とは異なります。学習者用デジタル教科書で可能となる学習として以下の内容が考えられます。

　①教科書の紙面を拡大して表示する（ポップアップやリフロー等を含む）
　②教科書の紙面にペンやマーカーで書き込むことを簡単に繰り返す
　③教科書の紙面に書き込んだ内容を保存・表示する

　学習者用デジタル教科書は，あくまでも紙ベースの教科書と同一の内容をデジタル化したものであり，動画・音声やアニメーション等のコンテンツは，学習者用デジタル教科書に含まれないことになっています。その他の学習者用デジタル教材と組み合わせて活用することで，上記した①〜③に加え，教科書紙面に用いられている語句や文，イラストに対応する英語の音声が聞けたり，場面や状況を表す映像やアニメが英語と共に流れたり，聞く音声のスピードが調整できたりなど，さらなる効果が期待される機能が見受けられます。
　一方，指導者用デジタル教科書は，学習者用デジタル教科書とデジタル教科書教材が合わさった機能を持っています。加えて，ワークシートやピクチャーカードなども，指導者が授業をするにあたって必要となる多様な支援ツールも含まれていることもあります。
　タブレットなどの端末を生かした活用も多くの教科で見受けられます。例えば，体育では，跳び箱を跳んでいる様子を動画で撮影し，その後見て跳び方の修正を行ったり，小学校の図工では，折り紙で作成した作品をコマ撮りし，それらの画像をつなぎ合わせて動画にしたりなどの実践がいろいろ出てきています。このように教科指導の在り方も今後変わってくるでしょう。

学校内での ICT 活用

　ICT 機器の活用は教科指導に関わることだけではありません。現在はインターネット環境も整備され，学校教育における様々な場面でも ICT が活用され始めています。

　現在多くの自治体，学校で導入が始まっているのが，統合型校務支援システムです。これは教員の働き方改革の観点からも導入が進められています。このシステムは，成績処理，児童生徒の出欠管理や健康診断票の管理，通知表や指導要録の作成，学校事務系など，これまで個々に存在していたものが，統合された機能を備えています。また，成績処理等だけなく，情報共有や掲示板機能なども備わり，教師の業務全般を実施するために必要となる機能が備わっており，今後多くの学校で校務 DX（Digital Transformation）の導入が進んでいくものと考えられています。

　また，保護者との連絡等も ICT の活用が進んできています。欠席連絡等これまで電話や連絡帳などを通じて行っていたことを，デジタル化し，メール等による連絡で可能となったり，学校だよりなどのお知らせなどもデジタル配信したり，など行っている学校も増えてきています。また，個人面談の希望調査などもこれまで紙面でのやりとりで行っていた煩雑になる作業もアンケートフォーム機能を使用して行うことで作業の負担が軽減されることにもなっています。

　このように教科の指導のみならず，学校教育全体に ICT が活用されている様子が見受けられます。しかし，全てのものを ICT 化，デジタル化すれば良いということでもなく，実際に会話を交わす，対面して対応する，など大切になってくる場面もあります。二項対立で捉えずに，アナログの良さとデジタルの強みを考えながら，いつ，どの場面で，どのツールを用いる方が効果的，効率的になるのかという判断をしっかりとしていくことが求められるのです。

6 Summary & Reflection

A Summary

Here is a brief summary of the readings. Fill in the blanks to check your comprehension.

ICT education is becoming more [1](　　　　　　) in school in Japan. It is rapidry being promoted by the GIGA School Plan. Children learn programming

and information literacy in elementary school and continue to improve these
²(   ) as they progress to middle and high school. One of the aims is
to create a better learning environment at school, and also ³(   ) students for Society 5.0. Using ICT, ⁴(   ) work will be much more effective. Group projects help students learn how to work well with ⁵(   )
and use their ICT skills to solve real ⁶(   ). Nevertheless, there are
challenges when introducing ICT, such as unequal access to technology and a
need for more qualified teachers. It is important to invest in ICT education to
ensure students are ready for the ⁷(   ) age and can take advantage of
its opportunities.

[B] Reflection

本章では，ICT 教育について学んできました。ICT 教育に関連する以下の語
句について，具体的な例をあげながら説明してみましょう。

	語　　句	説　　明
1	Information and Communi-cation Technology : ICT 情報通信技術	
2	GIGA School Plan GIGA スクール構想	
3	Information Literacy 情報活用能力	
4	Society 5.0 ソサイエティ5. 0	
5	Interactive Class 対話型授業	

Unit 14
CLIL

1 Warm-up Activities

A Choose the correct meaning for the following words or phrases using (1)
to (10) below.

(   ) necessary   (   ) mother tongue   (   ) citizen   (   ) lead to
(   ) respect   (   ) diverse   (   ) promote   (   ) coexistence
(   ) connect   (   ) recognize

---

1. the first language that you learn / acquire when you were a child：母語
2. relate to：〜と関係している
3. needed：必要な
4. to cause something to happen：〜につながる
5. very different from each other：多様な
6. someone who lives in a particular place：市民
7. the fact of existing together：共存
8. to help something develop：促進する
9. to accept that something is true：認める
10. the feeling you show when you accept differences：尊重する

B Read the following sentences, and check the box in front of each sentence
that describes you.

☐ 1. I have experience of learning a foreign language other than English in
the past.

☐ 2. I have heard of the word CLIL (/klɪl/).

☐ 3. I can explain the word CLIL.

☐ 4. It is exciting to study a subject other than English in English.

□ 5 . It is difficult to study subjects other than English in English.

2 Aural & Oral Activities

[A] Read the questions below. Then listen to Track 14-1 and decide whether each sentence is True (T) or False (F) according to the conversation.

1 . In yesterday's class, Steve learned about foreign language education in Europe. T/F

2 . According to Rie, students in Europe need to study three foreign languages. T/F

3 . In European schools, you can study whatever language you like. T/F

4 . Plurilingualism is an idea that learning many languages leads to a respect for diverse languages. T/F

5 . Steve wants to take English lessons based on a method that promotes plurilingualism. T/F

[B] Listen again and fill in the blanks. 🎧**Track 14-1** ▶

Steve : Oh no. I have another ¹(　　　　) test
next week. Why do I have to study English?

Rie : Yesterday in class we learned about foreign language education in Europe.

Steve : Do students in Europe study English at school?

Rie : A lot of them do. But that is not all. In Europe, you have to study your mother ²(　　　　) plus two foreign languages.

Steve : Two? Which languages do they have to study?

Rie : Languages used in the EU.

Steve : I wonder why do they study two foreign languages? I guess it is to make it easier for EU ³(　　　　) to communicate with each other?

Rie : That's right. Also, there an idea called 'plurilingualism'. Learning many languages leads to a ⁴(　　　　) for diversity in languages. It is said to ^{5}(   ) peace and coexistence of EU citizens.

Steve : Is it ^{6}(   ) to the history of conflict in Europe?

Rie :   Yes, it is. That is why people ^{7}(   ) the importance of foreign language learning. There are teaching methods and tools to promote 'plurilingualism'.

Steve : I wish I could take English lessons based on such a method!

$\boxed{\text{C}}$ Let's try 'Role-Play Shadowing'.

1 . Listen to the Track and check the pronunciation and meaning of each word and sentence.

2 . Try 'Role-Play Shadowing' using the Track with a partner.

3 . Change roles and repeat.

4 . Now role-play with a partner without the Track. Be sure to focus on using the appropriate intonation, rate of utterance and tone of voice.

$\boxed{\text{D}}$ Talk with a partner, and take turns asking and answering the following questions. Then, change partners, and ask and repeat.

1 . Do you have access to a foreign language everyday?

2 . Please list all the foreign languages you have seen or heard before coming to this class today.

3 . Are there any foreign languages you would like to learn?

4 . Tell us the reason for your answer to 3.

5 . What do you think are the advantages of learning more than one foreign language?

3 Reading Part

$\boxed{\text{A}}$ Vocabulary and Phrases

① stands for ～の略語である   ② integrate 統合する   ③ content 内容

④ refer to ～を示す   ⑤ confident 自信がある   ⑥ feature 特徴

⑦ cooperative learning 協働学習　⑧ autonomy 自律　⑨ motivation 動機づけ
⑩ cognition 思考　⑪ perspective 見方　⑫ encourage 促す
⑬ definition 定義　⑭ broaden 広げる　⑮ tolerance 寛容性

B True or False Questions

Read the following statements. After you have read the passage below, answer whether the sentences are True (T) or False (F) according to the passage.

1. CLT aims only to improve learners' linguistic competence. T/F

2. CLT is one type of CLIL. T/F

3. 5Fs framework describe the elements important in CLIL. T/F

4. There is a definition that uses cooperative learning instead of culture in the 4Cs. T/F

5. Competence to use more than one language is called plurilingualism. T/F

C Multiple Choice

After you have read the passage below, circle the correct statements in each group.

1. a. CLIL stands for Communication and Language Integrated Learning.

   b. CLIL stands for Cognition and Language Integrated Learning.

   c. CLIL stands for Content and Language Integrated Learning.

2. a. The first L (language) in CLIL refers to your native language.

   b. The first L (language) in CLIL refers to a foreign language.

   c. The first L (language) in CLIL refers to babbling.

3. a. Of the 4Cs, Culture has the least influence on Content, Cognition, and Communication.

   b. Of the 4Cs, Culture has the most influence on Content, Cognition, and Communication.

　　c. Of the 4Cs, Culture has more influence on Content, Cognition, and Communication than Community.

4 . a. When learning cooperatively, personal culture has the greatest influence on learning.

　　b. When learning cooperatively, only the culture of the whole community influences learning.

　　c. When learning cooperatively, cultures of the individual and the community influence learning.

5 . a. By learning more than one foreign language, students are expected to develop tolerance for their own languages.

　　b. By learning more than one foreign language, students are expected to develop tolerance for the cultures of others.

　　c. By learning more than one foreign language, students are expected to develop tolerance for the languages and cultures of others.

4 Reading Activities　　🎧Track 14-2 ▶

Read the following sentences. Listen to the Track, and read it again.

What is CLIL?

Communicative Language Teaching（CLT）is an approach that aims to improve learners' communicative competence through learner interaction. CLIL is a type of CLT. CLIL stands for Content and Language Integrated Learning. In CLIL, student learn content and language at the same time. Content refers to other subjects or themes, and language refers to a for-

stands for ～の略語である

integrate 統合する

content 内容

refer to ～を示す

eign language other than your native language. Do you think, "Learning subject content in English sounds difficult?" Don't worry. Even if you are not confident in your English, you may be interested in the content and tasks used in CLIL. Another feature of CLIL is cooperative learning. CLIL is said to have the power to increase learner autonomy and motivation.

There is a framework called the 4Cs that describes the elements that are important in CLIL. Those are Content, Cognition, Communication, and Culture. Try to integrate these elements in your teaching. Of the 4Cs, culture has the most influence. Culture includes awareness of one's own and other cultures, seeing the world from others' perspective, and developing an awareness to global citizenship. In order to develop these, we need to plan topics (content), language (communication), and activities that encourage deeper thinking (cognition). Some definitions use 'community' instead of 'culture' in the 4Cs. Community is learning through cooperation. When learning cooperatively, the culture of each member of the community influences what is learned. The culture of the community as a whole also influences learning.

Behind CLIL is the idea of plurilingualism. Plurilingualism is a competence of being able to use more than one language. By being a plurilingual, one can broaden his or her way of expressing oneself. Through learning many foreign languages, students are expected to develop tolerance towards other peo-

confident 自信がある
feature 特徴
cooperative learning 協同学習
autonomy 自律
motivation 動機づけ
cognition 思考

perspective 見方

encourage 促す
definition 定義

broaden 広げる

tolerance 寛容性

ple's languages and cultures. This can be done through education. Thus, when you conduct CLIL lessons, do not just think about language skills you try to teach. Try to remember the idea behind it.

5 Mini Lectures

1. 内容言語統合型学習 (CLIL)

CLIL とは

　言語学習において，コミュニケーション能力の向上を重視する教授法をまとめて，コミュニカティブランゲージ・ティーチング (CLT) と呼びます。その一つに CLIL があります。CLIL は，Content and Language Integrated Learning（内容言語統合型学習）の略語です。内容（テーマや教科）と言語（母語以外の言語）を統合して学習する指導法です。「英語だけでも難しいのに，英語で教科内容を学ぶなんて難しそう」と思われた方もいるかもしれません。小学生に CLIL による指導は可能なのでしょうか。

　CLIL では，学習者／児童が主役になります。児童は，興味のある内容について，様々なタスクを通して，協働的に思考を働かせながら学習します。英語力に不安があっても，学習内容やタスクには興味を持てるかもしれません。また，協働的に学ぶため，それぞれが得意なことを生かし，役割を担うことができます。このような点から，CLIL は，学習者の自律性や動機付けを高める可能性があると考えられています。本書のタイトルにも CLIL という用語が入っています。本書を通して，英語指導者に求められる知識／内容について，英語を通して学んでほしいと願っています。

小学校における CLIL の可能性

　平成29 (2017) 年に改訂された小学校学習指導要領の外国語の第 2　各言語の目標及び内容等には，指導計画を作成する際の配慮事項（以降，配慮事項）として，以下のような記述があります。

エ　言語活動で扱う題材は，児童の興味・関心に合ったものとし，国語科や音楽科，図画工作科など，他の教科等で児童が学習したことを活用したり，学校行事で扱う内容と関連付けたりするなどの工夫をすること。

この要点は，以下のようにまとめることができます。

・児童自身が英語を用いて意欲的にコミュニケーションを行うため，題材や活動を児童の興味・関心に合わせて選択する。
・他教科の学びを活かした活動を行う。
・学内にある様々な学習のためのリソース（学習指導要領解説では，絵本，物語，学校行事などが挙げられています）を活用し多様な活動を工夫する。

これらは，CLIL を実施するうえでも重要な視点です。
　小学校高学年の外国語の検定教科書においても，上記（エ）の配慮事項を反映し，CLIL の授業計画につながる題材や活動があります。例えば，社会科での学びにつながる歴史上の人物や世界の国々や，家庭科での学びにつながる食材を栄養素グループに分類する活動などです。文化的題材もたくさん収録されています。このように，他教科の学習内容や，文化に関するテーマを英語の授業において扱うことは，児童が英語を用いて主体的に知識を活用，思考，表現する場面を作り出します。
　これらを踏まえ，CLIL を行う際には，まず，検定教科書などの教材をはじめとした学内のリソースを見直しましょう。その際，CLIL を行う文脈について考慮しましょう。例えば，学校の目指す児童像，クラスサイズ，指導者と指導体制，児童の興味・関心や英語力などに応じて，カリキュラムや単元構成を考えます。その中で英語を使用する割合，扱うテーマなどの調整を行います。柔軟性は，CLIL の特徴の一つです。児童の実態に合わせ，行いやすい形で，少しずつ取り入れてみましょう。

４Ｃの枠組みと文化

　CLIL を行う際，授業の重要な構成要素をまとめた枠組みとして，「4C」が
あります。四つの C は，それぞれ，Content(学習内容)，Cognition(思考)，Com-
munication（言語），Culture（文化）を指します。これらを統合的に授業に組み
込むことで，効果的な CLIL の実践につながります。

　4C の中でもっとも影響力を持つのが，Culture（文化）です。Coyle（2007）
は，「文化は全てに浸透する」と述べています。CLIL には，CEFR の複言語主
義や複文化主義，異文化間能力育成の理念が影響を及ぼしています。そこで，
自文化・異文化への気づきや，他者の視点に立って世界を見ること，ひいては，
地球市民としての意識を育めるような指導が大切になります。4C の Culture(文
化) の代わりに Community（協学）を用いる説明もあります。協力しながら学
びを深めようとする際には，コミュニティの各構成員の持つ価値観や規範など
の文化や，コミュニティ全体の文化も影響を及ぼします。

2.　CLIL の４Ｃと実践

Content と Communication とその実践

　Mini Lectures 1 では，CLIL とその構成要素の枠組みである 4C の概念につ
いて学びました。そして，4C の内，Culture（文化）の定義と実践について学
びました。ここでは，CLIL 授業を計画する際のプロセスに沿って Content（内
容）と Communication（言語）について学びます。

Content（内容）

　まず，どんな教科内容や，テーマを取り上げるか検討します。学習内容は，
他教科ですでに学習した内容や，児童にとって身近な出来事などの中から選び
ます。4C の Culture（文化）に関わるテーマも CLIL に適しています。児童に
なじみのない内容を扱う際には，児童が既に持っている知識と関連付けして導
入するよう工夫しましょう。

　内容を検討する際，教科書を起点とすると，授業に取り入れやすくなります。
英語の教科書で扱う内容と，他教科や学校行事での学びを対照し，どのように

関連づけられるか検討しましょう。ここで，移行期用教材『We Can! 1』にある「She can run fast. He can jump high.」という単元を例にとり，どのような学習内容を扱えるか考えてみます。本単元の目標は，「自分や第三者について，できることやできないことを聞いたり言ったりする」ことです。ここに，小学校4年生の理科で学習した「動物の生活と種類」を結びつけることができます。地球市民意識を育てるため「絶滅危惧種」を取り上げてもよいですね。「can」という言語材料に対する理解を深めるため，「環境を守るために自分ができること」というテーマを扱うこともできます。このように，教科書の内容から様々な学習内容へと発展させることができます。

Communication（言語）

　CLIL は，コミュニケーションの育成を目指した教授法の一つです。Coyle, Hood and Marsh（2010）は，コミュニケーションをしながら学習する際に扱われる多様な言語を三つの観点から分類し説明しています。

①「学習の言語（Language of Learning）」

　内容を学習する際に，必要になる言語材料のことです。例えば，「動物のできること」について学習する場合は，動物を表す語や，できることを示す can，動作動詞などがこれにあたります。指導者は，必要になる「学習の言語」を分析し，どのように授業で扱うか，計画しましょう。柏木・伊藤（2020）は，児童を対象に語彙指導を行う場合は，授業の前半に，意味ある文脈の中で出会わせ，後半で絵カードやチャンツ（英語の単語や文をリズムに合わせて発音する学習法）で学ばせるとよいと説明します。

②「学習のための言語（Language for Learning）」

　児童が授業に参加するうえで必要になる言語材料のことです。例えば，活動に必要になる表現や，教師や友達に質問する表現などです。これらは，クラスルームイングリッシュとして普段から授業に取り入れましょう。

③「学習を通した言語（Language through Learning）」

　学習の過程で意図せず学ぶ言語のことを指します。学習者が学ぶ過程では，内容に関わる新出語や，活動で必要な語に加え，その学習者の表現したい内容に応じて，様々な語が必要となります。言語を使いながら学ぶ CLIL に特徴的な点だと言えます。「学習を通した言語」を事前に教師がすべて把握することは難しいですが，事前に，本課の学びに関連し，児童の興味・関心や，話したいと思うことを把握し，そこで活用できそうな既習表現を確認すると良いでしょう。

　CLIL の授業で未習の語句等が出てくる場合があります。その際，足場かけ（scaffolding）となる手立てを取ることが必要になります。足場かけは，自分一人では解決できない学びを一時的に支援することを指します。授業においては，教師や友達がその役割を果たすことがあります。この足場があることで，次のステップへと学びを進めることができるようになります。内容の理解やスキルの習得を助ける「足場」として，視覚教材（写真・地図・図表・ワークシートなど）も有用です。チャンツや歌なども活用できます。指導者は，英語で話すときの表情や声の調子，ジェスチャーも意識しましょう。

3．CLIL とその理念

Cognition（思考）

　最後に，Cognition（思考）について学びましょう。学習者の思考の育成を検討する際には，ベンジャミン・ブルーム（Benjamin Bloom）による教育目標分類が活用できます。表14-1は，その内，認知的領域に関する部分をまとめたものです。この特徴は，思考スキルを階層的に表しているところです。例えば，「動物の種類とできること」について学ぶ場合，動物の名前やその特徴（例えば，体温や住む場所，身体的特徴など）についての記憶や理解があると，特徴ごとの分類がしやすくなります。このように，高次の思考スキル（Higher Order Thinking Skills : HOTS）の学習を効果的に進めるには，低次の思考スキル（Lower Order Thinking Skills : LOTS）が必要になります。指導者は，児童の実態を把握

表14- 1　改訂版教育目標分類と動詞表

分類	思考スキル	動詞表（例）
Higher Order Thinking Skills : HOTS	Creating（創造）	考案する，統合する
	Evaluating（評価）	批評する，判断する
	Analyzing（分析）	分類する，分解する
Lower Order Thinking Skills : LOTS	Applying（応用）	応用する，利用する
	Understanding（理解）	比較する，説明する
	Remembering（記憶）	リスト化する，定義する

出所：Anderson and Krathwohl（2001）をもとに筆者作成。

し，どの思考スキルを育むと効果的か分析しましょう。その際，表14- 1 の動詞表が参考になります。

ヨーロッパにおける言語教育の理念

　Unit 5 でも述べましたが，ヨーロッパでは，過去の言語権の侵害や，戦争への反省から，複数言語の学習や異文化間能力育成が重視されています。

　CLIL という用語が開発された1990年代は，欧州連合（EU）の創立，域内の自由移動の拡大などに伴い，ヨーロッパ市民間におけるコミュニケーションの重要性がさらに高まっていた時期です。1995年に発表された EU 理事会による決議（Resolution of the Council）では，言語以外の分野を，外国語を用いて指導する教育を提供することと示されました。同年に発行された欧州委員会による『教育白書』（Comission of the European Communities, 1995）においては，教育目標の一つに域内の最低二つの外国語を学習することが掲げられています。

　CLIL の背後には，複言語主義の理念があります。複言語主義は，単に複数の言語を知っているということではありません。大木（2011）は，その目的を次の二つの側面から説明しています（表14- 2）。

　この理念は，欧州評議会の言語教育政策にも反映されています。代表的な産物には，CEFR（Council of Europe, 2001）があります。CEFR の目的は「ヨーロッパの言語教育のシラバス，カリキュラムのガイドライン，試験，教科書等々の向上のために一般的基盤を与えること（Council of Europe, 2001）」です。域内の移動機会が多い欧州では，学習や雇用等において，それぞれの言語能力を測る

表14-2　複言語主義の目的

複言語主義の目的	内　容
能力としての側面	複数の言語を使う能力を養成して，話し手の「言語レパートリー」を増やすこと
価値としての側面	言語の多様性を肯定的に受けいれることの価値に気づかせること

出所：大木（2011）をもとに筆者作成。

共通基盤の存在が不可欠です。CEFRでは，学習者の熟達度は六つの段階に分けられ，各レベルにおいて何ができるのか説明する能力記述文がcan-do形式で技能ごとに示されています。しかし，CEFRには複言語主義やICにかかわる記述が限定的であったため，補完するために「ことばと文化の複元的アプローチ参照枠（FREPA：Candelier, et al., 2012)」が発行されました。ここでは，IC要素の可視化が試みられています。また，IC育成を目標とする指導案も収録されています。また，2017年にはCEFRの補遺版が出版されました。ここでは，2001年版に不足していた異文化に関わる記述文が一部追加されました。CEFRの理念を言語教育の現場において実践することを目指し「ヨーロッパ言語ポートフォリオ（ELP)」も開発されました。

　このように，欧州では，EU市民同士の平和的共存のための言語教育の重要性が認識されています。そして，複言語主義や異文化間能力の育成を推進するため，様々な施策やツールなどが徐々に進展しています。CLILを実践する際は，単に英語教授法の一形態という理解ではなく，その理念にも意識を向けましょう。

6 Summary & Reflection

A Summary

Here is a brief summary of the readings. Fill in the blanks to check your comprehension.

CLIL is a type of Communicative Language Teaching (CLT) that aims to improve learners' communicative competence through learner interaction. CLIL [1]( )for Content and Language Integrated Learning. In CLIL, students learn ²(   ) (a subject or topic other than a foreign language) and language (a foreign language) at the same time.

There is a framework called the '4Cs' that describes what is important in CLIL. The 4Cs are Content, Cognition, Communication, and Culture. Of the 4 Cs, the most influential is Culture. It includes ³(   ) of one's own culture and that of others, as well as an awareness of global citizenship. When you plan your lesson, try to ⁴(   ) these elements.

Plurilingualism is the ability to use more than one ⁵(   ). By learning many foreign languages, students are expected to develop ⁶(   ) for other people's languages and cultures. It is believed that this can be developed through education. Therefore, the EU has developed a number of educational policies that ⁷(   ) these ideas.

B Reflection

本章では CLIL やその理念について学んできました。以下の語句について，具体的な例をあげながら説明してみましょう。

	語　句	説　明
1	Content and Language Integrated Learnig : CLIL 内容言語総合型学習 (クリル)	
2	4Cs 四つの C	
3	Scaffolding 足場かけ	
4	Higher Order Thinking Skills : HOTS 高次の思考スキル	

5	Lower Order Thinking Skills : LOTS 低次の思考スキル	

Unit 15
Cognitive and Non-Cognitive Ability

1 Warm-up Activities

A Choose the correct meaning for the following words or phrases using (1) to (10) below.

(   ) mindset   (   ) grit   (   ) self-efficacy   (   ) self-regulation

(   ) metacognition   (   ) recall   (   ) intelligence   (   ) cognition

(   ) self-actualization   (   ) competency

---

1 . an attitude someone has towards something：思考・態度

2 . to think about memories or the act of remembering：思う，想起

3 . a strength and determination to do something：やり抜く力・粘る力

4 . the ability to manage your thoughts and behaviors：自己調整

5 . the awareness of your own thoughts：メタ認知

6 . a realization of your talents and potentials：自己実現

7 . a belief in your capacity to take action towards a goal：自己効力感

8 . the capability of using knowledge and skills to achieve a goal：能力

9 . the ability to acquire knowledge and skills：知能

10. mental action or thinking used to learn or understand something：認知

B Read the following sentences, and check the box in front of each sentence that describes you.

☐ 1 . I do not give up easily on difficult tasks.

☐ 2 . I do not mind mistakes when I speak English.

☐ 3 . I am good at learning English.

☐ 4 . I usually plan my study schedule.

☐ 5 . I usually reflect on what I learned in a class.

☐ 6 . I have a long-term goal that I am trying to achieve

☐ 7 . I know the best way I can learn.

2 Aural & Oral Activities

A Read the questions below. Then listen to Track 15-1 and decide whether each sentence is True（T）or False（F）according to the conversation.

1 . Rie gets a second chance to take the test. T/F

2 . Steve is Steve's teacher. T/F

3 . Active recall means trying to remember something. T/F

4 . Writing a word many times is the best way to study vocabulary. T/F

5 . Active recall can be used for speaking practice too. T/F

B Listen again and fill in the blanks.   🎧**Track 15-1** ▶

Rie :   I was unable to get a good score on the test.

Steve : How did you study?

Rie :   I just wrote each word many times. I [1](   ) that was a good method to study, because my teacher said, "Keep trying".

Steve : Didn't your teacher give you advice on how to study better?

Rie :   Not really. He told me to do my best and [2](   ) me for trying.

Steve : I see. Maybe I can help you [3](   ) better.

Rie :   I'll take any [4](   ) I can get.

Steve : There are many ways to study. The most important method for memorization is called 'active recall', [5](   ) to research in learning.

Rie :   Active recall?

Steve : Yes, it is trying to remember what you studied. When you are only writing the word many times, you aren't using your brain or [6](   ) very well.

Rie :   I see. How can I do active recall?

Steve : Think of what you do during a test. You have nothing but your memory.

That means you are trying very hard to remember it, right?

Rie : Right.

Steve : So, put yourself in a ⁷(　　　　) to actively remember words.

Rie : I see. Active recall sounds like what I do when I try to speak English.

Steve : Now you are thinking! One aspect of speaking a second language is trying to remember the words you studied.

C Let's try 'Role-Play Shadowing'.

1. Listen to the Track and check the pronunciation and meaning of each word and sentence.

2. Try 'Role-Play Shadowing' using the Track with a partner.

3. Change roles and repeat.

4. Now role-play with a partner without the Track. Be sure to focus on using the appropriate intonation, rate of utterance, and tone of voice.

D Talk with a partner, and take turns asking and answering the following questions. Then, change partners, and ask and repeat.

1. What is a mistake you learned from the past?

2. What is your goal for this course?

3. What are your strengths in learning?

4. Are you good at finding the positives in others?

5. What is your best way to learn?

3 Reading Part

A Vocabulary and Phrases

① misinterpretations 誤解　② percentile 偏差値　③ coined 造語

④ dominate 支配　⑤ persistent 忍耐　⑥ citation 引用　⑦ op-ed 社説

⑧ other side of the coin 反面　⑨ coping mechanisms 対処法

⑩ rooted 〜に根差している

B True or False Questions

Read the following statements. After you have read the passage below, answer whether the sentences are True (T) or False (F) according to the passage.

1 . According to the passage, students have a growth mindset. T/F

2 . Growth mindsets are being taught in many classrooms in Japan. T/F

3 . The percentile-based system helps students learn better. T/F

4 . Most learners believe that if they *Gambaru* they will succeed. T/F

5 . Most learners possess effective learning strategies. T/F

C Multiple Choice

After you have read the passage below, circle the correct statements in each group.

1 . a. People with growth mindsets believe in the importance of persistent effort and have strategies to cope with failures.

   b. People with growth mindsets believe in the importance of only persistent effort to succeed.

   c. People with growth mindsets only believe in the importance of not giving up.

2 . a. Many Japanese teachers teach growth mindset strategies.

   b. Many Japanese teachers disagree with growth mindset strategies.

   c. Many Japanese teachers do not possess growth mindset strategies.

3 . a. The percentile-based system helps students persist.

   b. The percentile-based system does not help students persist.

   c. The percentile-based system teaches students various learning strategies.

4 . a. Okawa believes that schools are not praising students enough.

   b. Okawa believes that schools are praising students in the wrong way.

c. Okawa believes that schools should stop praising students.

5．a. A good title for the article is 'Japanese *Gambaru* Mindsets'.

b. A good title for the article is 'Japanese Growth Mindsets'.

c. A good title for the article is 'Japanese and Mindsets in the Classroom'.

4 Reading Activities

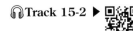Track 15-2 ▶

Read the following sentences. Listen to the Track, and read it again.

Gambaru, How?

rooted 〜に根差している

persistent 忍耐
coined 造語
misinterpretations 誤解

coping mechanisms 対処法

percentile 偏差値
dominate 支配

The word *Gambaru* is deeply rooted in Japanese culture and is often used when talking about studying. This culture may be viewed as students having growth mindsets, which many believe is simply a belief that to learn or grow one must give persistent effort. Carol Dweck, who coined the term 'growth mindset' informed educators about these misinterpretations. She reminded us it is not only the belief of persistent effort that is essential in successful learning, but also possessing effective learning strategies is necessary. Everyone would agree that learning and growing comes with many failures and challenges. Unfortunately, these coping mechanisms are usually not taught in school.

Kiyotake Okawa is an expert in the *Gambaru* culture. He argues that the percentile-based system is one reason *Gambaru* culture dominates education. This system places learners at a certain level by giving them a number. Therefore, it is easy to motivate students to *Gambaru*, or simply persist in their studies, so they can reach the next level, which is just one point away. Also, learners are often praised for persistent effort alone even though they do not achieve the next level. Thus, learners do not understand that *Gambaru* alone is insufficient and that learning strategies are the other side of the coin. Okawa eloquently illustrates this in the following Asahi Newspaper op-ed article from January of 1997 :

> My teacher repeatedly said, "Do your best." I thought I was doing my best, but no matter how much I tried, my teacher only says, "Do your best."

This citation reveals that the student does not have an effective learning strategy in coping with learning difficulties. The teacher does not teach the student how to learn. In situations like this, it is hard for students to develop growth mindsets or advance learning. In the worst case scenario, a student may grow a dislike for the subject or develop a fixed mindset.

other side of the coin　反面

op-ed　社説

citation　引用

5　Mini Lectures

1. 「学び」と認知機能の接点

「認知」とは

　「学ぶ」の語源は「真似る」から来ています。英語では「learn」ですが，この語源は「軌跡」なのだそうです。この意味が転じて「形が変わる」になり，やがて「行動の変容」を表すようになりました。

「教育」は江戸時代末期に「education」という英語の翻訳語として使用されるようになりました。教育するという意味の「educate」の語源はラテン語の「educere（引き出す）」にあるとされています。ここから何が汲み取れるでしょうか。一般的に「教育」とは，教師が設定した学習環境と学習課題を基に学習者が「学ぶ」ことを言います。これは別の角度から見ると，学習者の知っていることやできることを教師が増やしたり養ったりしている，とも言えます。つまり，教育とは子どもの可能性を「引き出すこと」とも言えるのです。

　また，「学ぶ」という行為は「認知機能」とも強い関わりを持っています。端的に言って，「認知能力」がなければ「学び」は起こり得ません。「認知機能」とは，情報を取得，処理，理解，適応するための脳の働きを表す言葉です。五感で様々な情報を取得するたびに認知作業が起こり，それは学ぶことにつながっていきます。心理学では，これらの知覚，判断，想像，推論，決定，記憶，言語理解等を包括して「認知」と呼びます。学校教育では，意識的・計画的にこの「認知」を通して学習者の態度や行動・価値観の変容を起こさせますが，このような変容は，普段の生活の中で自然に起こることでもあります。

「学び」とは

　最初に「学び」を研究したのはB.F. スキナー（Burrhus Frederic Skinner）だと言われます。スキナーは「学び」という「行動の変容」を，行動と行動がもたらす成果によって生まれるとする「オペラント条件づけ」という概念で説明しています。具体的には，教師が特定の刺激（褒美や罰など）を与えることにより，特定の「行動の変容」が形作られると言うものです。この考えに疑問を挟んだのが，J. ブルーナー（Jerome Bruner）です。彼は，特定の刺激だけではなく，その刺激や周りの環境との相互作用で「行動の変容」が起きると考えました。しかし，この両者のように「学び」を「認知」の側面からのみ捉えるのは十分ではないという考えも生まれてきます。それは，「非認知（能力開発や潜在能力）」の側面から「学び」を捉える方法です。

　心理学者の C. ロジャーズ（Carl Rogers）は，「学び」につながる「発見」や「理解」は内側から成り立つことであると述べ，学習者の成長と自己実現の過

程を重んじる「人間性理論」を提唱しました。これは，A. マズロー（Abraham Maslow）の「欲求階層理論」とつながるところがあるものです。学習者が自分の能力や可能性を利用し，基本的な欲求を段階的に満たすことで学び成長していく，という理論です。また，「学び」は受動的な行為ではなく，内的動機づけによる能動的な行為であるとも述べています。学習経験は，知識や技能などの認知的な物事だけではなく，自信などの非認知的な面にも影響を与えることになります。例えば，英語の授業で失敗を経験することで自信をなくし，「自分は英語が苦手」ということを学ぶ／メタ認知することが起こります。このように，認知された事は後の英語学習に何らかの影響を与える可能性がある，というわけです。

　この「学び」における認知・非認知の重要性を発展させたのが，R. ガニェ（Robert Gagne）です。ガニェは「学びは継続的な行為」であり，学習教材（刺激）や学習の場（環境）が同じであっても，結果には個人差が出ると述べています。従って，学びの個別化に焦点を当てた指導が必要だとガニェは考えました。このような「学び」に対する認識の発展を考えると，教師の役割は，学習者一人ひとりの複雑で異なる既存知識や技能に配慮し，学習目標を達成できるように様々な方法で指導することが必要になることが分かります。

多重知能の視点から

　H. ガードナー（Howard Gardner）は人間に九つの知性（自然的・音楽的・論理的数学的・実存的・対人的・身体運動的・言語的・個人的・空間的）があると述べています。この理論の根本にあるのは，学習者によって，ある種類の知性が強く，その他の知性は弱いということがあり，それぞれの能力には違いがあるという考えです。教師は，学習者の知性一つひとつを見出し，強い知性を活かしながら弱い知性を強化していく務めがあると言えるでしょう。適切な刺激と環境を与えることでそれを可能にします。複数の知性を発達させることで，学習者は多くの問題を自ら解決し，潜在能力を発揮することが可能になります。教師は，学習目標と学習課題を特定して，授業を慎重に計画する必要があります。また，年間の単元の計画を通して多くの知性を発揮できる活動を設けなければなりま

せん。活動や課題を設計する際，それぞれの学習者に合った学習内容や学習方法の選択ができるようにすることも，今後求められることになるでしょう。

2. 自己効力感が生まれる指導の大切さ「Yes, I can.」

自己効力感

　自己効力感とは，学習者が学習目標を達成するために必要な知識や技能を充分備えている，という信念のことです。この信念により，学習者は課題に取り組む際，失敗に直面しても挫折することなく，粘り強く学習意欲を持続させることができます。自己効力感が高い学習者には「効力期待（見返りの効用に満足できるかどうか）」と「結果期待（成功できると感じるかどうか）」があります。この二つの期待が高ければ，学習者は学びを継続することができます。一方，自己効力感が低い場合，無意識のうちに成功できないという信念を抱いてしまいます。これにより学ぶためのモチベーションが下がり，低い学習目標を定めてしまうことで自ら学びの機会を妨げたり，あるいは簡単に諦めることで継続を困難にしてしまったりします。

自己効力感に関する 3 つの要素

　学習者の自己効力感は，学習課題や授業中の活動ごとに異なります。いかなる環境の中においてもこの「できる（Yes, I can.）」姿勢を保つには，三つの要素が関係するとされています。その三つとは，①直接的達成経験（過去の成功体験），②代理的経験（自分と同じ条件にある生徒が目標を達成する場面を想像する），③言語的説得（目標達成できると励まされる）です。

　今までの成功や失敗の因果的根拠を自分自身に帰してしまう，という自己帰属という意識が含まれます。英語学習において失敗が多いと，学習者は「私は英語が下手だ」「私は英語学習が苦手だ」と感じます。これにより自己効力感は低くなっていきます。また，友達が自分の成功モデルとなるような姿を観察することを通して自分の可能性を高めることができたりします。さらに，エビデンスに基づいた科学的な説明やデータ等を示されることで可能性を信じることができるようになり目標達成に向けて取り組むことが可能となる場合もあり

ます。教師は，自己効力感が落ちないように工夫をすることはもちろん，学習者各自が成功体験を重ねられるよう授業を設計し，指導をすることが必要だと言えます。

Growth Mindset と Grit

　学習者の自己帰属は内部帰属と外部帰属に分けることができますが，どのように捉えるかにおいては，傾向として二つのマインドセットに分類されます。一つ目は，固定マインドセットをもつ学習者です。学力や知性は生まれつき備わったものであり，学習しても意味がないと考えます。つまり，元々頭が良い人とそうでない人が存在し，個人の特性や性格と関係があり，自分の力でどうにかできるものではないと考えるのです。そのため，おのずと学習意欲が貧弱になります。二つ目は，成長マインドセット（Growth Mindset）をもつ学習者です。こちらは，学力や知性は努力によって成長させることができるという信念を持っています。どちらのマインドセットを持っているかは，学習者によって違いますし，常に同じということではありません。例えば，英語の発音や文章作成能力など，学習領域によって，別々のマインドセットを持っていたりします。

　また，成長マインドセットは，「グリット／Grit（やり抜く力）」という概念に繋がります。行動と気質を含めた，目標に向けた長期的な忍耐力を指す概念です。グリットも学習に影響を与える非認知能力の一つです。しかし，学習者の認知能力（知識，自己帰属，学習能力）に依存している部分があるため，完全に非認知能力という分類はできないとする研究者もいます。研究が浅い分野ですが，トレーニングすれば高めることも可能だと少しずつ明らかになってきています。

　既に述べたとおり，教師は，学習者が自己効力感を高められる学びの場を提供する必要があります。効果的な学習方法を一緒に考えたり，設定する課題に工夫をすることで成功体験を持たせたりすることが可能になります。このように意識的にマインドセットを構築するための手助けとなる指導が肝要です。

　一例として，有名な科学者やスポーツ選手がどのように失敗や苦労を乗り越

え偉大な功績を達成したのかについて，話を聞き考える機会を持つことが考えられます。また，クラスメイト間で成功体験を話し合ったり，発表したりといったことでも可能です。一方で，学習に伴うストレスの対象法について学ぶ機会を与えることでも自己効力感を高められます。非認知能力は，学びの場で経験する「成功したという感覚」に大きく影響されるものです。「やればできる (Yes, I can.)」と思うことで，学習者は自ら新しいことを学び取り，問題解決に向けて成長していきます。

3. 成長マインドセットの育成
成長マインドセットトレーニングの実施と適切な教室文化の構築を

　授業を通して「成長マインドセット」を高めていかねばなりません。しかし，学習者が「頭」で，持続性と努力の重要性を認識することを理解するだけでは育ちません。失敗や課題を通して，状況に対処していく実際的な行動やコツを「体」を使って習得していくことが必要不可欠なのです。言い換えると，遭遇した状況に応じて最適な学習方法を，学習者自らが選択できる「思考と判断力」を身につけていくことが必要となります。要するに，成長マインドセットの育成に欠かせないのは，学習の自己調整能力の育成であり，そのための学習のトレーニング（自らの学習目標の設定，管理，評価）が必要であると言えるのです。もし学習者が，ある状況で不適切な学習方法を選択してそのまま継続してしまうなら，能力が高まることは期待できません。努力や粘り強さに対する盲目的な信念となってしまっていて，「固定マインドセット」が強くなるだけで終わりかねません。学びの過程に，困難や失敗はつきものです。学習者は壁にぶつかった時の対処方法として，様々な角度から問題を俯瞰して捉え，最も適切な解決策を探し出せる能力を培っていく必要があります。そこには，まず，自分にはいろいろな学習方法の選択肢がある，と知ることから生まれるはずです。

　学びの成果は教室文化に関係するところがあります。教室内の全員に共有された学習目標，能動的な学習形態，優れた学習課題と評価基準がある授業であっても，教室文化の状態次第で効果的な学びが止まってしまうケースも起こり得ます。例えば，一部の学習者のみに褒め言葉などの「報酬」を与えると，その

他の学習者の自己効力感が低下したり，「報酬」をもらったことで学習者は粘り強く学習する意義を無くしてしまったりする可能性すらあります。さらに，学習成果の共有や，思いや考えを発表し合うことに不安を感じる学習者がいたり，協働学習の方法や大切さが学習者たちに充分浸透していなかったりすると，学びの成果は期待できません。

学習方略とメタ認知能力

　成長マインドセットと表裏一体の関係を持つのはメタ認知能力と言えます。メタ認知能力とは，学習者の学習方略についての認知と言い換えられます。メタ認知能力が高い学習者は，集中する方法（気が散ったらどうするのかなど）や学習を効果的に持続する方法（ドリル的な練習を学習の中に効果的に含め，実施する計画を立てるなど）が身についています。また，学習が上手くいかない時，学習方法を変えるタイミングや，いつどのように協力を求めればよいか，その方法をも理解しています。協働学習の際等には，他の人の話を積極的に聞いたり，自らの理解不足を能動的に示したりすることができる学習者はメタ認知能力が高い，ということになります。その他にも，理解や能力の不十分さを気にしないで，間違いや失敗を恐れず好奇心のままに質問したり，挑戦したりする，といった特徴も見られます。

　「成長マインドセット」と「メタ認知能力」，この二つは，直接的，あるいは間接的に教え，高めていくことができます。直接的指導の一例としては，脳がどのような機能を持ち，どのような仕組みで成長するのかを教えるというものがあります。これは教室内に優れた学習文化を確立するための必須要素です。一方，間接的な育成は別の役割を担っています。学習者は各々能力において独自の適性を持っていますから，画一化された学習目標を達成するために必要な時間，労力，練習量はおのずと異なってきます。この複雑な状況に柔軟に対応していくために目標達成の際いくつかの評価基準を設けておく，といった工夫をすることで，間接的に成長を助けていくことができます。

　最後に，より優れた教室文化を築くためには教師の言動も大切です。近年注目され始めている励まし言葉や褒め言葉の「使い方」について考えてみましょ

う。例えば，「がんばって」や「Good job!」といった声掛けのみだと，成長マインドセットやメタ認知能力を育てるには不十分であるということです。声掛けの前後に，学習の意義を思い起こしたり学習改善につながる具体的な助言をしたりすることがとても重要になってきます。例えば，「Good job! 文と文の間にポーズを置いて話したからみんなが聞きやすかったね。」「大切な情報部分をゆっくりはっきりと話せば，気持ちがしっかり伝わるかもしれない。次は意識してやってみよう。がんばって！」といったふうにすることが効果的です。また，優れた教室文化を醸成することに役立つものとして，「教室のレイアウトの変更」もあります。机の並びや掲示物などを活動形態に応じて効果的に変えてみるのです。学習者が成長マインドセットの大切さを確認できるポスターや成長の軌跡が見られる成果物や作品，学級の強みや目指す学級像の掲示等を掲示することも効果的です。授業のはじめや終わりにクラスのモットーを声にして誓うといったこともできるはずです。

6 Summary & Reflection

A Summary

Here is a brief summary of the readings. Fill in the blanks to check your comprehension.

Humans are always thinking. This thinking is called ¹(　　　　　　). Students use this when they learn or complete a task. ²(　　　　　　) is often defined as thinking about thinking. The difference between these two is difficult to understand because they overlap. Cognition can be understood as problem-solving, attention, and decision making, or simply thinking about something. On the other hand, metacognition is when an individual has control over his cognition, or again thinking about his or her thinking. During learning, metacognition helps students plan, monitor, evaluate learning and even understand. For instance, imagine you are trying to solve a multiple-choice grammar question. Your cognition helps you answer the question using your memory, and metacognition helps you check your answer or understanding.

Metacognition is what helps you build confidence in learning. Confidence to complete a task successfully is called ³(   ). With this confidence, students can persist longer in their learning, which is called ⁴(   ). One important thing for the teacher to do is to help students build strategies to better their learning when they make mistakes or fail. Having these learning strategies is very important in learning. A student who understands the importance of persistence in learning and possesses learning strategies when facing challenges is said to have a ⁵(   ). On the other hand, not believing in the importance of putting effort in learning because intelligence is something people are born with is called a fixed mindset. One way to develop mindsets is to model or teach ⁶(   ) which is the planning, monitoring, and evaluating of learning. As students get better at doing these, their learning skills develop preparing them to be more successful.

B Reflection

　本章では，認知と非認知能力について学んできました。言語習得に関連する以下の語句について，具体的な例をあげながら説明してみましょう。

	語　句	説　明
1	Self-Efficacy 自己効力感	
2	Growth Mindset 成長思考	
3	Cognition 認知	

4	Self-Regulation 自己調整	
5	Metacognition 非認知	

クラスルーム・イングリッシュと Teacher Talk

　授業の進行や指示を与える際，クラスルーム・イングリッシュや Teacher Talk を多く用いることを心掛けましょう。映像，写真，絵，ジェスチャーなど理解の助けとなるヒントを与えながら繰り返し使用することで，教室で授業を進めるために用いられる英語に慣れながら，英語の自然なイントネーションや語句・文の強勢位置，英語の音の特徴，英語の語順や文構造にも触れる機会となるはずです。

1．クラスルーム・イングリッシュの重要性

（1）英語授業の雰囲気作りは，教師のクラスルーム・イングリッシュから

　日本人教師が当たり前のように英語を使う姿を見せることは，児童が英語を発話することへのハードルを低くすることにつながります。英語や英語の発音に自信がない日本人教師はクラスルーム・イングリッシュの使用を避ける傾向があるようです。早い段階で授業中の英語の使用に慣れておくことが大切だと言えます。全てを英語で進める必要はありません。できるところから，少しずつ始めてみましょう。使っているうちにうまくなっていくものです。

　教師が用いる英語は，学習者が理解できなければ，意味はありません。話すスピードや使用する英語も，適切な速さとやさしい英語を使うようにしましょう。日本人教師が ALT と英語を使う姿を児童に見せることも大切です。まずは，日本人教師が相手（ALT）に伝わるように工夫をしながら英語を使い，積極的に ALT とコミュニケーションをとる姿を見せることで，子どもたちにとって良きコミュニケーションのモデルになるからです。ネイティブスピーカーのような発音である必要はありません。あいづちやリアクション等を取り入れながら，自然なやりとりで，通じる発音であれば大丈夫です。そのためには，単語や文のアクセントの位置を間違わないように事前に確認をして発話練習をしておくことが肝心です。日本人教師が用いるあいづちやリアクションワーズに

触れることで，知らない間に子どもたちも少しずつ理解できるようになったり，だんだんと自分たちでも使用するようになったりするはずです。

（2）ALT とのT. T.（ティーム・ティーチング）を円滑に進めるために

ALT とのT. T. を行う際，クラスルーム・イングリッシュは効果的です。日本に来て間もない ALT であれば，日本語や英語の授業に慣れていません。日本人教師がクラスルーム・イングリッシュを用いることで，授業の進行状況や活動の内容，ALT に期待されていることや活動の流れを把握しやすくなります。ALT が自信を持って，積極的に授業に参加することができるようになるはずです。

（3）子どもの発話を支援する

子どもに発話を求める際，子どもが最初の言葉が出てこない場合があります。そのような場合，教師が，文の最初の一語，「I ....」「He....」「She....」等と言ってあげると声を出しやすくなります。また，うまく答えを出せない児童には，

T : What animals do you like?

S : ....

T : Animals. Dogs? Cats? Dolphins?

とヒントとなる例を言ってあげると良いでしょう。

児童の発話に対しては，文法の誤りや訂正をするのではなく，まずは，発話内容に反応するように心掛けましょう。グッドリスナーのモデルとしての日本人教師の役割も大切です。

S 1 : I like roly-poly.

T 　 : Oh, you like insects. Me, too. I like snails.

S 2 : I like soccer.

T 　 : Yes, I know. You are a member of the soccer team. 等

と反応してあげることで，聞き手を意識した発話をするようになります。児童の発話の支援となるように心掛けましょう。

（4）Recasting と Rephrasing を用いる

　児童の発話した文に文法的な誤りがある場合，誤りを直接的に訂正するのではなく，教師が正しい形で提示してあげる方法（recasting）を取るようにします。児童が「I like dog.」と答えた場合，教師は，「You like dogs.」と自然な反応をする中で正しい言語形式を与えてあげましょう。また，「I like bananas.」に「You like bananas.」と反応したり，「Your favorite fruits are bananas.」と別の表現を用いて Rephrasing したりすると良いでしょう。「I can play the guitar.」という児童には，「You are good at playing the guitar, Ken.」と既習表現を用いた Rephrasing で反応することで，英語を聞く機会を多く与えるようにすることが大切です。最初は難しく感じるかもしれませんが，徐々に慣れてくるはずです。

2．授業で英語を使う際の注意点
（1）児童が理解できる工夫をすることが肝心

　すべてを英語で行うことが優れた授業であるというわけではありません。児童の理解を超えるような英語は，逆に子どもに不安とストレスを与え，教師の自己満足で終わってしまいかねません。「英語のシャワーを浴びることが大切」と言われますが，理解できない英語のシャワーでは意味がありません。子どもが理解できる内容を，繰り返し少しずつ増やしながら使うことに意味があります。

（2）「コミュニケーション」のモデルとなる使用がポイント

　適切な声の大きさで，ゆっくり，はっきりと英語を話すことを心掛けます。意味を理解させるためのヒントになるジェスチャーや表情，イラスト，写真を見せたり，また日本語を用いたり，ALT と一緒にデモンストレーションをして見せたりすることがポイントです。学年が上がってきたらジェスチャーや日本語の使用を減らしていくことが可能になるはずです。覚えた英語をすらすらと発話使用とするのではなく，自然なコミュニケーションになるよう，児童に「語りかける」つもりで英語を使うことを心掛けましょう。

ALTとの対話活動は，本当のコミュニケーションの様子を見せる絶好のチャンスです。ALTの話にしっかりと反応しながら聞こうとする態度，相手に意思を伝えるための工夫を教師自身が示すことができるからです。ALTの発話が理解できない時は，分かったふりをせず，聞き返したり，確認をしたりして，丁寧な会話を持つ姿を見せるようにします。子どもたちが，将来，外国の人たちと協力をして仕事をする姿をイメージすることにもつながるはずです。

3．クラスルーム・イングリッシュの実際

　以下に，使えるようになってほしい基本的なクラスルーム・イングリッシュを状況・場面ごとに示します。実際に，教室で児童に語り掛けている姿をイメージしながら練習しましょう。教室で指導している教師になりきって，声や顔の表情，視線，ジャスチャーも使いながら何度も取り組むことで段々と自由に使えるようになってくるはずです。

（1）授業の始まり（あいさつ，授業の始め方）　🎧Tack 16-1 ▶

Hi, everyone! Hello, class!

Good morning, class! Good morning, everyone!

How are you? I feel good today.

I'm fine! I feel great! I'm OK.

I'm great! I'm good. Not bad.

I don't feel well. I don't feel good.

I have a cold.

I have a headache.

I have a stomachache.

How about you, Rika?

Take care of yourself.

（2）出席，天気，曜日の確認　🎧Track 16-2 ▶

Who's not here today? Who's absent today?

Is everyone here?

Is it sunny? How's the weather today? Yes, it's sunny!

Look! It's a beautiful day today. Is it Monday? Tuesday?

What day of the week is it today? What date is it today? It's July 4th.

Now let's begin!

Now let's start today's lesson!

Are you ready?

（3） ALT やゲストを迎える　　　　Track 16-3 ▶

We have a special guest today.

This is Ms. Harrington.

She is from Australia. Welcome to our class!

I'd like to introduce your new English teacher, Mr. Sweet.

He is from London. He can play tennis. He likes music.

It's question time. Let's ask him some questions. Anybody?

（4） 聞き返す　　　　　　　　　Track 16-4 ▶

Excuse me? Say that again, please.

Sorry? Slowly, please.

Pardon? Would you repeat that again, please?

Sorry, I couldn't hear you well. Would you please speak more slowly?

（5） 子どもをほめる　　　　　　　Track 16-5 ▶

Great! Well done! Super!

Wonderful! Excellent! Awesome! Close!

Good job, Yui! You did a good job!

I'm proud of you. Good try.

（6）活動の指示 Track 16-6 ▶

First, let's watch a video.

Let's sing a song together.

Let's listen to a CD.

Look at the blackboard.

Now, let's go on to the next activity.

Please listen to your friends carefully.

Make good eye contact.

Any volunteers? Raise your hands.

Naomi, please come up to the front.

Let's play a gesture game. Guess what they are doing.

Guess what I'm doing / drawing.

Attention, please.

Point to the correct picture.

Color the circle yellow.

OK! Calm down!

Stop talking, please.

Listen to me, please.

（7）グループ分け，ワークシート／カードの配布 　Track 16-7 ▶

Let's make pairs. Now, we'll make three groups.

Let's make groups of three.

You join team A, please.

Here are some cards. Take one and pass the rest.

Please pass out these worksheets. Can you help me, Miki? Thank you.

The group leaders, please come to the front with the correct card.

One point for group A! Group B is the winner.

Group A gets one point. The winner is group A! Congratulations!

You all did a good job.

228

（8）活動の評価，振り返り，授業を終える 🎧Track 16-8 ▶

Natsue, you were a very good listener.

Aya was a very good speaker.

Yumi, your voice was very clear.

Wataru and Sayaka made good eye contact.

Naoko had a great smile.

Akira and Mari, you communicated very well.

Are you finished?

Please write your name on your paper.

Put away your pencils.

It's time to say good-bye.

Let's say "Thank you." to Mr. Baker.

We had a great time! Did you have a good time?

Class, let's give Ms. Brown a big hand!

You did a very good job.

Good-bye, everyone! See you next time!

See you next week! See you soon!

Have a good day!

Have a wonderful weekend.（morning / afternoon / week）

Small Talk

　授業・単元の始まり等にその日の活動や単元の内容と関連する子どもに身近な話題について英語で話したり，ALT との自然な会話を見せたりするようにします。既習の言語材料を中心に用いることで，復習となるだけでなく，新しい単元やその日の活動への興味・関心を持たせることが可能になります。実態に応じて，簡単な質問をして答えさせたり，児童同士での会話活動を持たせたりすることでウォームアップとして実施することも可能です。「前の時間に学んだことを覚えていますか？」と質問するのではなく，Small Talk を通して思い出させ，英語の授業の雰囲気作りを行います。

　以下，具体的な内容に関する Small Talk の例を見てみましょう。Small Talk で話した内容について，既習の英語表現を用いて質問をして答えさせたり，児童同士の会話活動につなげたりします。児童の英語力に応じて，写真やジェスチャーを用いながら，話すスピード，間の取り方，話し方を工夫することが大切です。児童に身近な事や教師，授業，学校行事，地域の事，単元に関連するトピックを選びます。

（1）「夏休みの思い出」の単元の授業で ALT と行う Small Talk 例

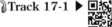🎧Track 17-1 ▶

ALT : How was your summer vacation?

　　　I enjoyed my summer vacation.

　　　I went to a beach on July 1st.

　　　I enjoyed beach volleyball.

　　　It was great. I ate three hot dogs on the beach.

HRT : Oh, you played beach volleyball on the beach. Nice.

ALT : How about you? Did you enjoy your summer vacation?

HRT : Yes.

ALT: Good. What did you do during your summer vacation?

HRT: I went to my grand parent's house in Tokushima.

I watched the fireworks with my grandparents.

I ate rainbow shaved ice.

ALT: Wow. It sounds nice.

（２）お気に入りの物について伝え合う単元で ALT と行う Small Talk の例

🎧Track 17-2 ▶

HRT: Bruce, let's talk about our favorite things.

My favorite thing is this family photo.

Look at her. This is my sister. She is a music teacher.

ALT: Oh, that's a good picture.

HRT: What is your favorite thing?

ALT: My favorite thing is this cell phone. It was a birthday present from my parents.

HRT: You can talk to your family and take pictures and movies.

ALT: Yes, I usually use this phone to take pictures.

I have a lot of photos of beautiful Japanese things, like a Japanese garden, *kimono, hina ningyo, ukiyoe*, and others.

HRT: Great! Can I see your photos later?

ALT: Yes, sure. Why not?

（３）小学校の思い出について伝え合う単元で児童と行う Small Talk 例（６年生）

🎧Track 17-3 ▶

HRT: You are about to finish your elementary school days soon.

How was your life at elementary school?

You have many good memories.

What is your good memory of your elementary school days?

Student A : Our school trip to *kamakura*.

HRT :　　Our school trip to *kamakura*. Why?

Student A : I had a good time with my friends! I saw the great Buddha.

　　　　　　It was big. I enjoyed visiting beautiful temples and shrines, too.

HRT :　　I see. I like *Zeni Arai Benten* shrine. How about you, Tanaka-San?

Student B : Well…, sports day. I enjoyed running in a relay race.

HRT :　　Yes. You can run fast, Tanaka-San. You are a good runner.

　　　　　　I'm glad to hear about your good school life memories.

（4）将来の夢について扱う単元で ALT と行う Small Talk 例

🎧Track 17-4 ▶

HRT : Today, we are going to talk about our dreams

　　　for the future.

（昔の写真を見せながら）

　　　Look at this. This is a picture of my 12th birthday party.

　　　I was a 6th grader. I liked sports, and I wanted to be a teacher.

ALT : That's great! So, you are a P.E. teacher now.

HRT : How about you? What did you want to be in the future?

ALT : When I was 12 years old, （子どもの頃の写真を見せながら）

　　　I wanted to be a vet or a zookeeper. I liked animals.

HRT : Oh, interesting! A vet! A zookeeper!

　　　What do you want to be now?

ALT : I want to make AI robots in the future.

HRT : Wow, that's great!

ALT : I like science and robotics. I want to be a scientist.

HRT : Great. You can do it!

ALT : Thank you.

（5）中学校に入学したらやってみたいことを扱う単元で行う HRT の Small
　　Talk 例　　　　　　　　　　　　　　🎧Track 17-5 ▶ [QR code]

（小学生のころの写真を見せながら，当時の気持ちに
なって話をすることを伝える。）

HRT : Hello everyone. I'm Jun.

I like P.E. I can jump high. I want to join a basketball team in junior high
school. What club do you want to join?

I want to be a music teacher. I like singing.

I want to enjoy a chorus contest in junior high school.

What event do you want to enjoy?

I hope you have a happy junior high school life.

Make your dreams come true.

引用・参考文献

Unit 2

金森強（2019）『小学校英語科教育法──理論と実践』成美堂.

Ortega, L.（2009）*Understanding Second Language Acquisition.* Hodder Education.

Unit 3

中央教育審議会（2016）「幼稚園，小学校，中学校，高等学校及び特別支援学校の学習指導要領等の改善及び必要な方策等について(答申)(中教審第197号)」https://www.mext.go.jp/b_menu/shingi/chukyo/chukyo0/toushin/1380731.htm（2023年12月10日閲覧）.

星野由子・清水遥（2019）「小学校外国語・外国語活動で扱われるカタカナ語──日本語と英語の語義の比較分析を通して」『小学校英語教育学会誌』19（1），pp. 117–129.

文部科学省（2017）『小学校学習指導要領（平成29年告示）解説　外国語活動・外国語編』https://www.mext.go.jp/content/20220614-mxt_kyoiku02-100002607_11.pdf（2024年3月7日閲覧）.

Aitchison, J.（2012）*Words in the Mind : An Introduction to the Mental Lexicon.*（4th ed.）West Sussex : Wiley-Blackwell.

Unit 4

東後勝明監修，御園和夫編（2009）『英語発音指導マニュアル』北星堂.

Celce-Murcia, M., Briton, D. & Goodwin, J. M.（2010）*Teaching Pronunciation : A Reference for Teachers of English to Speakers of other Languages*（3rd ed.），Cambridge University Press.

Jenkins, J.（2015）*Global Englishes*（3rd ed.），Routledge.

Kirkpatrick, A.（2007）*World Englishes : Implications for International Communication and English Language Teaching.* Cambridge University Press.

Morley, J.（1999）"New Development in Speech /Pronunciation." *As We Speak,* 2（1），pp. 1–5.

Zielinski, B.（2008）"The Listener : No Longer the Silent Partner in Reduced Intelligibility." ScienceDirect. *System,* 36（1），pp. 69–84.

Unit 5

カルトン，フランシス（2015）「異文化間教育とは何か」西山教行・細川英雄・大木充

編『異文化間教育とは何か――グローバル人材育成のために』くろしお出版.

中山夏恵・栗原文子（2019）「学習指導要領の改訂に伴う小学校外国語教材の変化――異文化間能力育成の観点から」JACET教育問題研究会会誌『言語教師教育』6（1）, pp. 94-112.

文部科学省（2017）『小学校学習指導要領（平成29年告示）解説　外国語活動・外国語編』https://www.mext.go.jp/content/20220614-mxt_kyoiku02-100002607_11.pdf（2024年3月7日閲覧）.

Byram, M.（1997）*Teaching and Assessing Intercultural Communicative Competence*, Clevedon : Multilingual Matters Ltd.

Council of Europe（2001）*Common European Framework of Reference for Languages : Learning, Teaching, Assessment*. Cambrdige : Cambridge University Press.

Mercer, S., Hockly, N., Stobart, G., & Gales, N. L.（2019）*Global Skills : Creating Empowered 21st Century Citizens*. Oxford University Press.

Mourão, S.（2022）"Picturebooks and Reading Aloud in the Early English Language Classroom," *The ICEGuide:A Handbook for Intercultural Citizenship Education through Picturebooks in Early English Language Learning*, https://icepell.eu/（2023年8月28日閲覧）.

Unit 6

アレン玉井光江（2010）『小学校英語の教育法――理論と実践』大修館書店.

白畑知彦ほか（2019）『英語教育用語辞典第3版』大修館書店.

文部科学省（2018）『小学校学習指導要領解説　外国語活動・外国語編』開隆堂出版, p. 78, 130.

Unit 7

大西泰斗・ポール・マクベイ（2011）『一億人の英文法――すべての日本人に贈る「話すため」の英文法』ナガセ.

文部科学省（2018）『小学校学習指導要領解説　外国語活動・外国語編』開隆堂出版.

Anderson, J. R.（1983）*The Architecture of Cognition*. Cambridge. MA : Harvard University Press.

Unit 8

髙橋和子（2022）「小学校検定教科書における児童文学――教員養成への示唆」『教育学部研究紀要』12, pp. 1-15, https://meisei.repo.nii.ac.jp/?action=pages_view_main&active_action=repository_view_main_item_detail&item_id=2867&item_no=1&page_id=13&block_id=114（2023年3月11日閲覧）.

東京学芸大学（2017）「文部科学省委託事業『英語教員の英語力・指導力強化のための

調査研究事業』平成28年度報告書」https://www2.u-gakugei.ac.jp/~estudv/report/index
html（2024年3月7日閲覧）.

文部科学省（2018）『Let's Try! 1　指導編』東京書籍.

Hunt, P.（2001）*Children's Literature.* Blackwell, p. 3.

Opie, I., & Opie, P.（Eds.）（1997）*The Oxford Dictionary of Nursery Rhymes*（2nd ed.）. Oxford UP, p. 252.

Unit 9

稲田豊史（2022）『映画を早送りで観る人たち――ファスト映画・ネタバレ―コンテンツ消費の現在形』光文社.

外山滋比古（2002）『外山滋比古著作集二――近代読者論』みすず書房, p. 103.

松居直（2003）『絵本のよろこび』日本放送出版協会, p. 45.

文部科学省（2018）『Let's Try! 2　指導編』東京書籍, p. 38.

Carter, R., & Nash, W.（1990）*Seeing through Language : A Guide to Styles of English Writing.* Basil Blackwell, pp. 38-42.

Hunt, P.（2001）*Children's Literature.* Blackwell, p. 289.

Wilde, O.（1966）"The Happy Prince," in *Complete Works of Oscar Wilde.* Harper & Row, pp. 285-291.

Unit 10

国立教育政策研究所（2020）「学習指導要領を理解するためのヒント」https://www.nier.go.jp/05_kenkyu_seika/pdf_seika/r02/r020603-01.pdf（2023年3月22日閲覧）.

文部科学省（2018）『小学校学習指導要領解説　総則編』東洋館出版社.

文部科学省（2018）『中学校学習指導要領解説　総則編』東山書房.

文部科学省（2019）『高等学校学習指導要領解説　総則編』東洋館出版社.

Unit 11

金森強（2019）『小学校英語科教育法――理論と実践』成美堂.

Unit 12

白畑知彦ほか（2019）『英語教育用語辞典第3版』大修館書店.

文部科学省（2018）『小学校学習指導要領解説　外国語活動・外国語編』開隆堂出版.

Krashen, S. D., & Terrell, T. D.（1983）*The Natural Approach : Language Acquisition in the Classroom.*

Unit 13

文部科学省（2018）「学校教育法の一部を改正する法律」https://www.mext.go.jp/a_men u/shotou/kyoukasho/seido/1407716.htm（2023年3月22日閲覧）.

文部科学省（2018）『小学校学習指導要領』東洋館出版社.

文部科学省（2018）『中学校学習指導要領』東山書房.

文部科学省（2019）『高等学校学習指導要領』東山書房.

文部科学省（2020）「GIGA スクール構想の実現へ」https://www.mext.go.jp/content/202 00625_mxt_syoto01-000003278_1.pdf（2023年3月22日閲覧）.

Unit 14

大木充（2011）「『ヨーロッパ言語共通参照枠』（CEFR）に学ぶ外国語学習の意義」大木充・西山教行編『マルチ言語宣言——なぜ英語以外の外国語を学ぶのか』京都大学学術出版会.

柏木賀津子・伊藤由紀子（2020）『小中学校で取り組むはじめての CLIL 授業づくり』大修館書店.

文部科学省（2017）「小学校学習指導要領（平成29年告示）解説　外国語活動・外国語編」https://www.mext.go.jp/content/20220614-mxt_kyoiku02-100002607_11.pdf（2024年3月7日閲覧）.

文部科学省（2018）『新学習指導要領対応小学校外国語教材　We Can! 1　指導編』.

Anderson, L. & Krathwohl, D. R., (2001) *A Taxonomy for Learning, Teaching, and Assessing : A Revision of Bloom's Taxonomy of Educational Objectives.* Longman.

Candelier, M., Camilleri-Grima, A., Castellotti, V., de Pietro, J-F., Lőrincz, I., Meißner, F-J., Noguerol, A., & Schröder-Sura, A.（2012）*A Framework of Reference for Pluralistic Approaches to Languages and Cultures.* Council of Europe Publishing.

Comission of the European Communities（1995）*White Paper on Education and Training Teaching and Learning – Towards the Learning Society*（教育白書）, https://op.europa.e u/en/publication-detail/-/publication/d0a8aa7a-5311-4eee-904c-98fa541108d8/language-e n（2023年8月28日閲覧）.

Council of Europe.（2001）*Common European Framework of Reference for Languages : Learning, Teaching, Assessment.* Cambrdige : Cambridge University Press.

Council of Europe.（2018）*Common European Framework of Reference for Languages : Learning, Teaching, Assessment Companion Volume with New Descriptors*, https://rm.coe.int/ cefr-companion-volume-with-new-descriptors-2018/1680787989ELP（2023年8月28日閲覧）.

Coyle, D.,（2007）"Towards a Connected Research Agenda for CLIL Pedagogies". *The International Journal of Bilingual Education and Bilingualism* 10（5）, pp. 543–562.

Coyle, D., Hood, O., & D. Marsh.（2010）. *CLIL : Content and Language Integrated Learn-*

ing. Cambridge : Cambridge University Press.

クラスルーム・イングリッシュと Teacher Talk
金森強（2019）『小学校英語科教育法——理論と実践』成美堂.

索　引

(＊は人名)

≪**執筆者紹介**≫（50音順，＊は編著者）

＊金森　強（かなもり　つよし）

> 文教大学教育学部教授
> 担当：はじめに，Unit 2，Unit 4,
> 　　　クラスルーム・イングリッシュと Teachers Talk, Small Talk

髙橋　和子（たかはし　かずこ）

> 明星大学教育学部教授
> 担当：Unit 8，Unit 9

田辺　尚子（たなべ　なおこ）

> 文教大学教育学部教授
> 担当：Unit 6，Unit 7，Unit 12

中山　夏恵（なかやま　なつえ）

> 文教大学教育学部教授
> 担当：Unit 3，Unit 5，Unit 14

西村　秀之（にしむら　ひでゆき）

> 玉川大学大学院教育学研究科准教授
> 担当：Unit 10，Unit 13

福田　スティーブ利久（ふくだ　すてぃいぶとしひさ）

> 文教大学教育学部教授
> 担当：Unit 1，Unit 11，Unit 15

〈本文イラスト〉
　赤川ちかこ

〈音源制作〉
　長橋一明

CLIL で習得する　小学校英語指導の基礎

2024年5月1日　初版第1刷発行　　　　　　　　　〈検印省略〉

定価はカバーに
表示しています

編 著 者　　金　森　　　　強
発 行 者　　杉　田　啓　三
印 刷 者　　藤　森　英　夫

発行所　株式会社　ミネルヴァ書房
607-8494 京都市山科区日ノ岡堤谷町1
電話代表　（075）581-5191
振替口座　01020-0-8076

亜細亜印刷・新生製本
ISBN978-4-623-09708-1
Printed in Japan

ICT を活用する　新しい時代の教育方法　　　　　　　　　　A 5 判・228頁
佐藤仁・伊藤亜希子・和田美千代 編著　　　　　　　　　　本　体 2400円

対話的で深い学びのある道徳科の授業をつくる　　　　　　　B 5 判・272頁
牧崎幸夫・広岡義之・岩井晃子・杉中康平 編　　　　　　　本　体 2800円

総合的な学習の時間の新展開　　　　　　　　　　　　　　　A 5 判・248頁
広岡義之・林泰成・貝塚茂樹 監修　釜田聡・松井千鶴子・梅野正信 編著　本　体 2400円

特別支援教育と障害児の保育・福祉　　　　　　　　　　　　A 5 判・336頁
──切れ目や隙間のない支援と配慮　　　　　　　　　　　　本　体 2800円
杉本敏夫 監修　立花直樹・中村明美・松井剛太・井上和久・河崎美香 編著

事例で読む学級経営　　　　　　　　　　　　　　　　　　　A 5 判・244頁
田中耕治 監修　岸田蘭子・盛永俊弘 編著　　　　　　　　本　体 2500円

不登校の理解と支援のためのハンドブック　　　　　　　　　A 5 判・312頁
──多様な学びの場を保障するために　　　　　　　　　　　本　体 2600円
伊藤美奈子 編著

幼児期の教育と小学校教育をつなぐ　　　　　　　　　　　　B 5 判・176頁
幼保小の「架け橋プログラム」実践のためのガイド　　　　　本　体 2500円
湯川秀樹・山下文一 監修

━━━━━━━━━━━━━━ ミネルヴァ書房 ━━━━━━━━━━━━━━

https://www.minervashobo.co.jp/